Documents in Contemporary History

*General editor*
Kevin Jefferys
Faculty of Arts and Education, University of Plymouth

# British economic development since 1945

*Documents in Contemporary History* is a series designed for sixth-formers and undergraduates in higher education: it aims to provide both an overview of specialist research on topics in post–1939 British history and a wide-ranging selection of primary source materials.

*Already published in the series*

Alan Booth *British economic development since 1945*

Stephen Brooke *Reform and reconstruction: Britain after the war, 1945–51*

Kevin Jefferys *War and Reform: British politics during the Second World War*

Ritchie Ovendale *British defence policy since 1945*

*Forthcoming*

Stuart Ball *The Conservative Party, 1940–92*

John Bayliss *Anglo-American relations: the rise and fall of the special relationship*

Steven Fielding *The Labour Party since 1951*

Sean Greenwood *Britain and European integration since the Second World War*

Harriet Jones *The politics of affluence: Britain 1951–64*

Jane Lewis *Women in post-war British Society*

Rodney Lowe *Britain's post-war welfare state*

Scott Lucas *The lion's last war*

Panikos Panayi *The impact of immigration*

Harold L. Smith *Britain in the Second World War: a social history*

Sabine Wichert *The integrity of their quarrel: Northern Ireland, 1939 to the present day*

Chris Wrigley *British trade unions since 1945*

Documents in Contemporary History

# British economic development since 1945

Edited by
Alan Booth
*Senior Lecturer in Economic and Social History, University of Exeter*

Manchester University Press
Manchester and New York
*distributed exclusively in the USA and Canada by St Martin's Press*

*Published by* Manchester University Press
Oxford Road, Manchester M13 9NR, UK
*and* Room 400, 175 Fifth Avenue, New York, NY 10010, USA

*Distributed exclusively in the USA and Canada*
*by* St. Martin's Press, Inc., 175 Fifth Avenue, New York,
NY 10010, USA

*British Library Cataloguing-in-Publication Data*
A catalogue record for this book is available from the British Library

*Library of Congress Cataloging-in-Publication Data applied for*
British economic development since 1945 / edited by Alan Booth.
p. cm. — (Documents in contemporary history)
Includes index.
ISBN 0-7190-4502-9. — ISBN 0-7190-4503-7 (pbk. : alk. paper)
1. Great Britain—Economic conditions—1945- I. Booth, Alan, Ph.D. II. Series,
HC256.5.B724 1996 95-4964
330.941'085—dc20 CIP

ISBN 0 7190 4502 9 *hardback*
0 7190 4503 7 *paperback*

First published 1995

99 98 97 96 95 10 9 8 7 6 5 4 3 2 1

Typeset in Linotron Sabon
by Servis Filmsetting Ltd, Manchester
Printed in Great Britain
by Bell & Bain Ltd, Glasgow

# Contents

# List of tables and figures

## Tables



## Figures

# Preface

This book is designed to fill a gap in the bibliography for students of modern economic history. There are relatively few collections of documents which meet the specific needs of economic historians and, to the best of my knowledge, none concentrates exclusively on British economic performance since 1945. A-level and first-year undergraduate students are also unintentionally excluded from much of the rapidly increasing literature on Britain's post-war relative economic decline. Contemporary economic history is a province populated by both applied economists and economic historians and its literature is increasingly characterised by the use of ever more sophisticated models and the specialised lexicon of professional economists. Some care has been taken to explain economic terminology in the text of the introduction, but where space is limited or a more detailed account is needed, an asterisk * will direct the reader to an entry in the short glossary at the end of the book. Economic terms in the extracts themselves are elucidated in footnotes at the bottom of the relevant page. No economic history can ignore the quantitative dimension, but an effort has been made to meet the needs of the target readership by trying to present the data in user-friendly forms, especially in graphs and charts. There are tables in the introduction (and even a rather large, messy one, with too many explanatory footnotes) but I hope that quantitative information will be accessible to all and will encourage those with the mistaken belief that they are 'number-blind' to tackle tables and figures in the more advanced studies discussed at the end of the book.

Alan Booth
Witheridge
November 1994

# Acknowledgements

For permission to reproduce excerpts the editor and the publishers would like to thank the following: the Controller of Her Majesty's Stationery Office for permission to reproduce Crown copyright material (1.1, 1.3, 2.1–6, 2.8–13, 3.2–3, 3.6, 3.8, 4.2, 4.4–9) and material subject to parliamentary copyright (2.7, 3.10, 5.1), Lady Brenda Clarke (3.2), the Organisation for Economic Co-operation and Development (1.2, 1.6, 2.14, © OECD, 1962, 1991, 1987, *OECD Economic Surveys, United Kingdom*), Guardian Newspapers ltd (1.4, 2.15–16, © *The Guardian*), the Rt Hon. the Lord Lawson and Transworld Publishers Ltd. (1.5, © 1992 Extracted from *The View from No 11* by Lord Lawson. Published by Bantam Books. All rights reserved), the *Economist* (2.17, 3.4, 3.11, © *The Economist*, 19 March 1994, 20 May 1967, 26 September 1992), the Royal Economic Society and Macmillan Press Ltd (3.1, © the Royal Economic Society 1979), the Rt Hon. the Lord Wilson of Rievaulx (3.5, 5.3, reproduced by permission of David Higham Associates Ltd), the Bank of England (3.7), the Rt Hon. Lord Healey of Riddlesden (3.9, reproduced by permission of Michael Joseph Ltd and Peters, Fraser and Dunlop Group Ltd), Times Newspapers Ltd (4.1), the Trades Union Congress (4.3), Newspaper Publishing PLC (4.10), Caroline Maudling (5.2), the Fabian Society (5.4), the Institute of Economic Affairs (5.5, 5.10), the Rt Hon. the Lord Lever of Manchester (5.6), Correlli Barnett and Macmillan Press Ltd (5.7), Professor R. E. Rowthorn (5.8), the Centre for Policy Studies (5.9), the *New Statesman and Society* (5.11), Professor Angus Maddison (Tables 1,4, material by permission of Oxford University Press) and Professor C. H. Feinstein (Tables 2–3, 5–6, Figure 1).

# Chronology of events

This is not a comprehensive record of events. Major economic events occur with breathtaking frequency and speed. It is intended as a selective chronological reference for the extracts on the following pages.

| | |
|---|---|
| | **1945** |
| September–December | Negotiations in Washington for post-war loan from US to UK government. |
| | **1947** |
| 1 January | National Coal Board takes over nationalised coal mining industry. |
| February–April | Fuel crisis causes cuts in coal and electricity supplies, lay-offs and short-time working. |
| 5 June | Marshall Aid announced but does not begin to flow until well into 1948. |
| July | Convertibility crisis as US loan agreed in 1945 depletes rapidly. |
| | **1948** |
| 1 January | British Transport Commission takes over nationalised railway, road haulage, canal and coach industry. |
| February | First post-war incomes policy announced, and lasts until October 1950. |
| 1 April | British Electricity Authority takes over nationalised electricity industry. |
| | **1949** |
| 18 September | Sterling devalued from £1 = $4.03 to £1 = $2.80. |

| | |
|---|---|
| | **1951** |
| 29 January | Massive rearmament programme announced in preparation for Korean war. |
| | **1955** |
| 27 October | Autumn (emergency) budget marks the first stop-go episode unaffected by war, reconstruction or rearmament. |
| | **1957** |
| 25 March | EEC 'six' (France, Germany, Italy, Benelux) sign Treaty of Rome. |
| 19 September | Another major 'stop' package of economic policy measures but imposed on an economy which was already slowing in order to prevent speculation against sterling. |
| | **1958** |
| 14 November | Britain's proposal for a large European free-trade area, without federal political overtones, rejected by France. |
| | **1961** |
| 25 July | First 'pay pause' (short-term freeze on pay rates) announced. |
| 8 August | TUC and employers invited to join a new National Economic Development Council, which begins to discuss the implications of faster growth for the UK economy. |
| 10 August | Britain applies to join EEC. |
| | **1962** |
| 9 May | Publication of NEDC exploration of the implications of a 4 per cent growth rate. |
| | **1963** |
| 9 May | Maudling's 'dash for growth' budget. |
| | **1964** |
| 15 October | General election victory for Labour under Harold Wilson after a campaign fought on the need for economic modernisation. Establishment of new Department of Economic Affairs in |

| | |
|---|---|
| | Whitehall to promote faster growth. New government reveals large balance of payments deficit on current account resulting from Maudling 'dash for growth'. |
| | **1965** |
| 16 September | Department of Economic Affairs publishes the National Plan, which establishes a growth target of approximately 3.8 per cent per annum. |
| | **1966** |
| 20 July | Emergency budget puts paid to growth strategy outlined by National Plan. |
| | **1967** |
| 11 May | Britain applies for membership of the EEC. |
| 18 November | Sterling devalued from £1 = $2.80 to £1 = $2.40. |
| 27 November | France rejects British application to join the EEC. |
| | **1968** |
| 13 June | Publication of the Donovan report. |
| | **1969** |
| 5 October | Department of Economic Affairs abolished. |
| | **1970** |
| 18 June | General election returns a Conservative government committed to less state intervention and entry to the EEC to promote faster growth. |
| | **1971** |
| 28 February | Major provisions of the Industrial Relations Act come into force and immediately provoke industrial conflict. |
| | **1972** |
| January | Crude total of numbers unemployed passes one million for the first time in the post-war period. |
| 21 March | 'Barber budget' as government expands the economy to boost the growth rate |

| | |
|---|---|
| | and states that fixed exchange rates will not be allowed to thwart growth strategy. |
| 23 June | Sterling allowed to float. |
| 6 November | Another 'pay pause' begins. |
| | **1973** |
| 1 January | Britain officially joins EEC. |
| October | OPEC doubles oil prices and cuts production and doubles prices again within months of the first announcement. |
| | **1974** |
| 4 March | General election which returns a Labour government committed to further nationalisation to modernise British industry. |
| 4 December | New government takes the first steps which lead to the nationalisation of British Leyland Motor Corporation and in the following year it nationalises Chrysler UK, a second ailing motor manufacturer. |
| | **1976** |
| June | Sterling crisis begins and leads to a steady fall in sterling's value on the foreign exchanges. The government negotiates a loan from other central banks, cuts public expenditure, and raises both interest rates and taxes. |
| 28–9 September | Prime Minister tells his party conference that Keynesian policies are no longer viable and government applies for a conditional loan from the IMF. |
| 15 December | Chancellor of the Exchequer presents to Parliament the 'letter of intent' which signifies government acceptance of the IMF's tough terms for its loan. |
| | **1978** |
| 26 September | Engineering Union (AUEW) makes official a strike at the Ford Motor Company, the first in the 'Winter of Discontent' which lasts until March 1979 |

| | |
|---|---|
| | and mainly involves public sector workers. |
| | **1979** |
| 4 May | Conservative government takes office committed to break away from the post-war consensus to improve economic performance. |
| June | OPEC again raises oil prices in stages, so that the price of a barrel rises from $14 in June 1979 to $36 in early 1981. |
| June | Interest rates rise above 14 per cent and stay above that level for twenty-one months, the toughest period of dear money for at least 150 years. |
| July–June 1980 | GDP falls by 4 per cent, the biggest contraction of the economy in a twelve-month period since 1921–22. |
| | **1981** |
| 10 March | Deflationary budget (taxes raised, public expenditure cut) to curb monetary growth at a time of economic recession signifies strength of monetarist influence within Treasury. |
| | **1982** |
| February | Shares of Amersham International sold to the public – the first privatisation issue. |
| 18 October | The government's second Employment Act introduced and is the first of many to weaken trade union power substantially. |
| | **1984** |
| November | Sale of half the government's shareholding in British Telecom. |
| | **1985** |
| December–April 86 | Oil prices fall from $29 to $10 per barrel. |
| | **1986** |
| December | British Gas privatised. |
| | **1987** |
| 14–28 October | World stock markets crash but without serious adverse effect on world economic |

| | |
|---|---|
| | progress. The loosening of monetary policy in Britain contributes to increasingly inflationary boom. |
| | **1990** |
| April-June | Slump begins. |
| 5 October | Britain enters the Exchange Rate Mechanism of the European Monetary System. |
| | **1991** |
| January–December | Output falls by 2.5 per cent, one of the largest falls in a single year since the war. |
| | **1992** |
| March-April | First signs of recovery as private consumption begins to grow slowly. |
| 16 September | 'Black Wednesday' – Britain leaves the Exchange Rate Mechanism and sterling's value falls quickly in currency markets. |
| 31 December | Single European market completed. |

# Introduction

In 1950 the average Briton was wealthier than the inhabitant of any other European country except Switzerland, and Britain's living standards were fifth highest in the world. Over the next four decades the British economy grew at a rate faster than ever before, so that by 1989 real living standards* were more than twice as high as they had been in 1950. By that time, however, Britain had slipped to twelfth place in the living standards league table; Britain has experienced *relative* economic decline. In the period since 1870 the British economy had grown at roughly two-thirds the average rate of the richest industrial economies (Table 1), though economic historians offer sharply differing views over the timing, dynamics and significance of this comparatively slow growth.[1] To its most severe critics, however, the British economy has endured a century of relatively weak growth.

***Table 1*** **Growth rates of real GDP per head, 1870–1989** (annual average compound growth rates) (per cent)

| *Country* | *1870–1913* | *1913–50* | *1950–73* | *1973–89* |
|---|---|---|---|---|
| France | 1.3 | 1.1 | 4.0 | 1.8 |
| Germany | 1.6 | 0.7 | 4.9 | 2.1 |
| Japan | 1.4 | 0.9 | 8.0 | 3.1 |
| UK | 1.0 | 0.8 | 2.5 | 1.8 |
| USA | 1.8 | 1.6 | 2.2 | 1.6 |
| Average of sixteen OECD countries[a] | 1.4 | 1.2 | 3.8 | 2.1 |

*Note*
(a) Australia, Austria, Belgium, Canada, Denmark, Finland, Italy, the Netherlands, Norway, Sweden and Switzerland plus the countries listed.

*Source* Angus Maddison, *Dynamic Forces in Capitalist Development: A Long-Run Comparative View*, Oxford, 1991, p. 49.

This 'British disease' has been one of the most intensively studied problems in modern social science, but no authoritative diagnosis has yet emerged. At the time of writing the British economy is slowly emerging from a very dramatic cycle of boom and bust. No one can say with any confidence whether this cycle has changed the underlying growth rate,* nor even whether any effect is more likely to improve or harm future performance. This is not an invitation to abandon hope. In order to attempt an intelligent review of available evidence, however, it is necessary to know something about the strengths and weaknesses of the sources upon which competing accounts are based.

## Some general words of warning

*The limitations of official statistics.* Statistics are the most basic source material for an economic historian and the official statistics collected and published by the Central Statistical Office (CSO) appear hard, exact and precise – quintessentially 'factual material'. However, British official statistics are not without their critics. Harold Macmillan (extract 5.1) complained about delays in producing figures. Denis Healey (extract 3.9) questioned the reliability of balance of payments estimates. The CSO's standards of accuracy are set by a policy-making timetable and not by academic discourse. As more information becomes available previous statistics are revised, and the CSO's first estimates of the balance of payments are notorious for substantial later revisions – published figures as far back as 1945 were substantially revised by the CSO as late as 1981 – and so even figures for the 1960s onwards need to be handled with care.

Statistical problems go deeper. In the 1980s *forecasts* of total output became more unreliable (extract 5.11), in part because CSO figures of national product* became less certain. In theory, national product can be measured in three different ways, which should all give the same result. In the 1980s these three methods of counting began to diverge widely. As will become clear, analysis of economic performance over the whole post-war period hinges upon debates about what happened in the 1980s. It is unhelpful that basic data for that decade are so uncertain. Statistics may also show only part of what they purport to explain. The competitive strength of British manufacturing is a central part of the 'British disease' and there are different ways to define and measure the competitiveness (extract 2.10). None of these takes any account of so-called 'non-price' factors, such as design, quality and reliability, where British manufacturers have allegedly been very weak. It is impossible to know by how much British competitive weakness results from price or non-price factors. Statistics can also be highly political. A storm arose in the 1980s when the CSO made a series of changes in the way unemployment was counted. All these changes except one reduced 'official' unemployment at a time when employment was falling. In short, official statistics must be treated carefully.

*The limitations of scientific economics.* Equally fundamental problems occur in assessing economists' explanations of the growth process. Economists like to claim that their discipline has the qualities of a 'science', similar to, say, engineering. It is a set of discovered truths about how the world operates and not, like history and other social sciences, a way of thinking about how the world may work. In the process, the discipline has become much more quantitative, theoretical and standardised. Unfortunately, even highly regarded economists doubt whether these hard, quantitatively based theories can explain the causes of economic growth in real economies, in real time, in the real world (extract 5.11).

The most damaging blow to the claims of economics to offer 'scientific' insights into the growth process was the eruption of doctrinal disputes in the profession in the 1970s. These disagreements are considered in greater depth in the last section of this introduction, but it is worth noting here that the authority of economists was dented when strong disagreements arose between Keynesians, who claimed that the decisive influences were exclusively on the demand side,* and monetarists, who insisted that the focus on demand was misleading and only the supply side* really mattered. The new focus on the supply side in the 1970s gave added force to growth accounting,* a method of analysing the causes of growth. Growth accounting allocates the causes of changes in national product between changes in the quantity of inputs (the supply of labour or capital) and the efficiency with which these inputs are used. The former quantity term is known as *factor inputs*, and the latter efficiency term is usually known as *total factor productivity*. It is obvious that the quantity of labour and capital are supply-side phenomena, but the efficiency term, total factor productivity, is frequently presented as 'the pace of technical progress', which is also a supply-side variable. This approach dominates much recent writing on economic growth. Its leading exponent is Angus Maddison, and his studies of growth in the developed economies since the nineteenth century are essential reading on this topic.[2] Similarly, the main academic treatment of British growth since the 1850s also uses the growth accounting technique.[3] For all its academic achievements, growth accounting has not been without its (very strident) critics. The basic formulation – change in national product is equal to the sum of the changes in total factor inputs and total factor productivity – is an *identity*, it is always true and cannot therefore readily illustrate the *causes* of fast or slow growth. The results produced by growth accounting have tended to show that the important changes occur not in total factor inputs (which are relatively easy to explain) but in total factor productivity (which is impossible to explain with any degree of conviction). Finally, in order to be accurate in attributing the causes of growth between inputs and efficiency, the method makes extremely demanding assumptions about the nature of the economic system which no one realistically believes that the real world can match. Accordingly, growth accounting is extremely controversial, despite the impressive scholarly credentials of its leading exponents.

In this rather unhelpful state of affairs, new energies have been diverted to understanding the growth process. Three very different avenues deserve attention. First, the tendency for the gap between the living standards of national economies to narrow since 1950 has rested, according to some economists, upon *convergence* of national productivity levels. At the core of this hypothesis is the proposition that if a 'lead' nation opens a large productivity gap over its rivals, there is a potential for faster growth among all other nations if best industrial practices can be transmitted from the 'leader' and absorbed by the 'followers'. However, convergence theorists have found it difficult to isolate the precise factors which encourage or discourage the transmission of technology, in its widest sense, from one country to another. *New growth theory* has been developed within the neoclassical framework to try to show why investments in physical or human capital can lead to persistent differences in national growth rates instead of to diminishing returns. It appears very relevant to the British case, where investment levels appear comparatively low and work-force skills are underdeveloped.

However, these theories have not been empirically tested and their main policy conclusion appears not to apply in the British case (extract 5.10). Finally, *institutional* explanations have recently been given greater economic theoretical coherence. There has long been a British institutional tradition, which has been especially strong in applied economics (extracts 5.5 and 5.6) and industrial relations. But in more recent times the US economist Mancur Olson, has used neoclassical economic concepts to create a general theory of institutional behaviour.[4] The essence of Olson's argument is that the longer a country enjoys social and political stability the more likely it is to develop a network of institutions which block fast growth. British social scientists have, however, been largely unimpressed both by Olson and by other institutional explanations which have essentially derived their model of optimal or desirable institutional behaviour from US experience.[5]

This excursion into the history of economists' treatment of the main determinants of economic growth has had a single objective; to reinforce the message of extract 5.11 that economists cannot claim to have constructed a 'scientific' *theory* of economic growth. Economic growth is too complex for current theories to explain.

*Limitations of objectivity.* If economic historians have particular problems in dealing with quantitative sources and organising material on the basis of disputed theoretical insights, they share all historians' problems of the partiality of literary sources. Documentary materials are produced in a definite economic, social and political context and the interpretations therein are inevitably filtered through and coloured by that context. The vast majority of the extracts dealing with industrial performance and the working of the labour market, for example, were written by men or by committees dominated by men. The growing importance of female labour during the post-war years is largely overlooked; the identification of 'the worker' as masculine is almost all-pervasive. There are many accounts of the problems of skilled, male manual workers but there is a dearth of good primary sources through which to study the female labour market, the most rapidly growing sector of employment (extract 4.7 and Figure 7 below). The bias within sources can be subtle but extremely powerful nonetheless.

Unfortunately, many of the extracts collected in this volume were written under conditions which emphasised rather than minimised the risk of partiality and bias. Throughout most of the period since

1945 the British economy has been perceived as performing less well than the competition. With British economic performance apparently failing so consistently, the temptation to point the finger of blame has been almost irresistible. There has inevitably been a 'political' dimension to some analyses of Britain's economic performance. This point is most obvious in the contributions from politicians. It is only to be expected that a Conservative Minister should emphasise how much better the economy has performed than under Labour (extract 1.5); that Labour politicians should describe the intellectual driving force of their opponents as 'mumbo-jumbo' (extract 3.9); that Conservatives should blame the unions (extract 5.2) and Labour criticise financial interests (extracts 5.3 and 5.6). The known or anticipated biases of sources may even be useful. The status of *The Times* as the authoritative (at least until the 1980s) voice of 'the establishment view' is extremely helpful if the object is to discover how far new ideas or values have penetrated into the policy-making elite (extract 4.1). By the same token, it is instructive to counterpose the attitudes taken by journals with pronounced and different doctrinal positions – in this case, the strongly anti-monetarist economic pages of *The Guardian* and the equally vigorous pro-market approach of *The Economist* on the significance of 'deindustrialisation' (extracts 2.16 and 2.17).

But there are also cases where partiality and the politicisation of opinion are less obvious and thus more difficult to accommodate. Government publications, for example, have long been regarded as a significant source of all modern historians – and, incidentally, form the largest single source for extracts in this volume. It is surprising how 'political' command papers, seemingly the most authoritative of all government publications, can be, as two examples will demonstrate. The first concerns a white paper, *A Statement on the Economic Considerations affecting Relations between Employers and Workers* (Cmd 7018), which the Attlee government issued in January 1947. Ministers had become concerned about wage demands and inflation and produced a draft white paper (reproduced in part as extract 4.2) which was overtly critical of the unions. The TUC representatives objected very strongly and fought tenaciously for changes. The final text can only be described as 'timid', not at all what the government wanted to say. The 1985 white paper *Employment: A Challenge for the Nation* (reproduced in part as extract 4.9), on the other hand, is precisely what the government wanted to say but is an exercise in propaganda and blame-shifting rather than authoritative analysis. The text explains the rise of unemployment since 1979 exclusively in terms of previous bad practices. It ignores completely the strong arguments (see extract 1.4) that mistakes in economic policy caused the large rise in unemployment. Not all white papers are so transparently propagandist but it would be equally unrealistic to expect any white paper to be totally free of partiality. The user must beware and proceed with caution.

These same warnings apply to other government publications. The *Economic Progress Reports* also tread the narrow dividing line between information-giving and propaganda. The discussion of the impact of microelectronics (extract 2.11), for example, takes a managerial view of the impact of technological change on the labour market (compare the union approach to similar questions in extract 4.3). The calculations of the impact of oil on GNP (extract 2.12) include no estimates of the negative impact of oil on manufacturing output via movements in the exchange rate. Partiality remains even when analyses are produced by apparently representative bodies, like the Anglo-American Council on Productivity, which operated from August 1948 to June 1952. Its main activity was to sponsor study visits to the USA by groups from British industry and to publish the reports which the visits generated. The reports covered an enormous range of British industry and give a telling insight into the ways in which British production methods and organisation compared with those of the USA. The cotton textile team report (from which extract 2.3 is taken) was dominated by employers, with limited union representation. Its ordering of the causes of higher US productivity is especially interesting. At the top of the list are three factors which may broadly be described as critical of the attitude of labour towards effort, technical change and work study. At the bottom of the list are factors, such as the level of investment and the maintenance of capital equipment, which may broadly be described as managerial functions. If this priority list is compared with problems identified in another industry (motor cars), at another time (the mid-1970s), but with similar problems of poor competitiveness (extract 2.7), the priority order is reversed, with low investment levels given as the cause of poor competitiveness. The divergence *may* reflect variations in conditions between the two industries, but it *may* also be caused by the differences in the structure of authorship.

This may seem a depressing catalogue of shortcomings in the primary sources on post-war British economic performance. The end result, however, is to leave economic historians in approximately the same position as other historians when dealing with source materials. It is essential to be sensitive to the strengths and weaknesses of evidence. It matters little whether that evidence is literary or quantitative. Even figures can be unreliable, despite the impression of exactness and precision which they are wont to create. Nor is the inability of theoretical economics to provide effective, scientific answers to questions which economic historians would like to pose (What determines the rate of economic growth? What determines the level of employment and unemployment?) an excuse to abandon theory completely. At the very least, the status of economists' understanding of the causes of growth is no worse than that of the theoretical insights which historians have happily drawn from other social sciences. The failure of sociology and politics to create an edifice of 'scientific' theory comparable to the laws of physics or engineering has not stopped historians from applying theories from these social 'sciences' in an effort to make sense of the historical world. Finally, it is an essential aspect of the historian's craft to be alive to possible biases and blinkered perspectives in sources. All historians have to make judgements about the reliability of evidence and build these assessments into the ways in which material is weighed. No sources are totally value-free. No written history is value-free. The obvious implication is that historians have to be scrupulously careful both about what they read and about what they write.

## A context for the extracts

*Aggregate performance.* The most important measure of long-run economic performance is the rate of economic growth. The most reliable estimates of growth are taken from peak years of the trade cycle (extact 1.5) which have comparable levels of economic activity and exclude periods in which special, temporary conditions prevail. Thus most surveys of post-war growth omit the later 1940s, when there were real problems in switching from a pattern of wartime to a pattern of civilian demand (extract 1.1), not least because most civilian industries had lacked investment for the duration of war (extracts 1.1, 2.1). Shortages persisted for a long time after 1945, especially of food (extract 2.2), but 1951, the peak of the first post-war trade cycle,* is usually taken as the start of 'normal' peacetime conditions. Thereafter there have been seven complete trade cycles: 1951–55, 1955–60, 1960–64, 1964–68, 1968–73, 1973–79, 1979–90. The first five cyclical peaks occurred in years of full employment, and the period 1951–73 is often treated as a single unit. However, reliable comparisons become much more difficult after 1973.

The first difficulty concerns what is termed the extent of capacity utilisation.* The trade cycle peak of 1979 was weaker than either 1973 or 1990, and so does not entirely fulfil the requirements for accurate measurement. Adjustments can be made, but are controversial. Secondly, there is the question of what to do about North Sea oil and gas, which accounted for only 0.01 per cent of national product in 1975, but a substantial amount thereafter (extract 2.12), rising to 7 per cent in 1984. This has been a windfall gain for the British economy (the benefits greatly exceed the cost of extraction) and economists frequently estimate national product with and without North Sea production. Finally, we have already seen that official estimates of national product in the 1980s are uncertain. With these qualifications in mind, Table 2 gives estimates of British growth rates since 1951 with and without adjustments for the 'low peak' of 1979 and with and without North Sea output. Table 2 reinforces and elaborates the picture which emerged from Table 1: growth was faster during the long boom (1951–73) than it has been

***Table* 2 Growth of UK GDP,[a] 1951–88** (annual percentage growth rates)

| *Period* | *Unadjusted peak years* | *Adjusted peak years*[b] |
|---|---|---|
| 1951–55 | 3.0 | 2.9 |
| 1955–60 | 2.5 | 2.3 |
| 1960–64 | 3.4 | 3.4 |
| 1964–68 | 2.8 | 3.0 |
| 1968–73 | 3.2 | 3.0 |
| 1973–79 | 1.4 (0.9)[c] | 1.8 (1.3)[c] |
| 1979–88 | 2.2 (2.2)[c] | 2.1 (2.0)[c] |

*Notes*

(a) Using the CSO's average measure of GDP.

(b) Calculated using the average of the peak and the preceding year.

(c) Excluding extraction of mineral oil and natural gas.

*Source* C. H. Feinstein and R. C. O. Matthews, 'The growth of output and productivity in the UK: the 1980s as a phase in the post-war period', *National Institute Economic Review*, 133, 1990, p. 79.

***Table 3*** **Growth of GDP,[a] factor inputs and TFP, 1924–88** (per cent per annum)

| *Period* | *GDP*[a] | *Labour input*[b] | *Capital input*[c] | *TFP* |
|---|---|---|---|---|
| 1924–37 | 2.2 | 1.5 | 1.5 | 0.7 |
| 1951–55 | 2.8 | 0.5 | 2.3 | 1.8 |
| 1955–60 | 2.5 | –0.4 | 2.6 | 2.1 |
| 1960–64 | 3.4 | –0.2 | 3.4 | 2.5 |
| 1964–68 | 2.6 | –1.5 | 4.1 | 2.5 |
| 1968–73 | 2.6 | –0.9 | 3.7 | 2.2 |
| 1951–73 | 2.8 | –0.5 | 3.2 | 2.3 |
| 1973–79[d] | 1.3 | –0.8 | 0.1 | 0.7 |
| 1979–88[d] | 2.0 | –0.6 | 2.0[e] | n.a.[e] |

*Notes*
(a) Excluding North Sea output.
(b) Labour is measured in terms of worker/hours. Improvements in labour quality appear in TFP.
(c) Capital is measured gross.
(d) Figures for 1979 are adjusted for the low peak of the cycle. See Table 2 for explanation.
(e) The depth of the slump of 1979–82 has made estimates of both the capital stock and total factor productivity growth in the 1980s unreliable.

*Sources* R. C. O. Matthews *et al.*, *British Economic Growth, 1856–1973*, Oxford, 1982, pp. 208, 548; Feinstein and Matthews, 'The growth of output', pp. 79, 84, 86.

since 1973, but the period of slower growth comprises a phase of substantial deceleration between 1973 and 1979 and an improvement thereafter which remains even after the exclusion of North Sea output and the complications of measuring the 1979 cyclical peak.

Growth accounting can help identify the sources of economic growth. As noted in the previous section, this methodology attempts to analyse the extent to which increases in output have been caused by additional *factor inputs* and *total factor productivity*. Table 3 shows that labour input has fallen throughout the post-war years; increases in the number of workers have been more than offset by reductions in hours worked. The main sources of growth, especially during the long boom, have been higher investment and faster total factor productivity growth. As we have seen, total factor productivity growth comprises all those factors which allow inputs of labour and capital to be used more efficiently. They may include: technical progress – both in machinery and in business organisation; the quality and flexibility of both managers and workers; the quality of the goods and services which they produce; the incentives to increase effort; the ability of firms to undertake research and

***Table 4*** **Comparative levels of productivity, 1870–1989** (US GDP per man hour=100)

| *Country* | *1870* | *1913* | *1938* | *1950* | *1973* | *1987* | *1989* |
|---|---|---|---|---|---|---|---|
| France | 60 | 54 | 54 | 44 | 76 | 94 | n.a. |
| Germany | 61 | 57 | 46 | 33 | 71 | 80 | 82 |
| Japan | 24 | 22 | 23 | 14 | 46 | 61 | 64 |
| UK | 114 | 81 | 63 | 56 | 64 | 80 | 78 |
| USA | 100 | 100 | 100 | 100 | 100 | 100 | 100 |
| Average of 15 OECD countries[a] | 77 | 61 | 45 | 46 | 69 | 79 | n.a. |

*Note*

(a) France, Germany, Japan, the UK and the eleven countries listed in note (a) of Table 1.

*Source* Maddison, *Dynamic Forces in Capitalist Development*, pp. 53, 274–5.

development. But in the 1970s total factor productivity growth slowed to rates which had prevailed in the inter-war years and there were almost no net additions to the capital stock. British economic performance between 1973 and 1979 was dire. The recovery after 1979 reflects above all a recovery in investment.

Tables 2 and 3 may help us understand better the rhythms of British post-war economic growth, but they cannot do much more than hint at the causes of relative decline. For a more penetrating insight into *relative* performance, we need *comparative* figures. This exercise is inherently more difficult, as it requires the conversion of different national data into a common standard, but reliable international data are now available. In assessing comparative economic performance, productivity measures are usually regarded as the most appropriate yardstick. The most common productivity measure is *labour productivity*, dividing total national product by the total number of workers, but economists now prefer to compare levels and rates of growth of output *per hour worked*. This method takes account of national differences in the 'normal' hours of work, but data on hours worked are not always very reliable, so inaccuracies can arise. The best available estimates are given in Table 4, which compares the level of output per hour in each economy with that achieved by the USA in the same year. The table also uses the most accurate techniques available for converting values in one currency into another, by *purchasing power parities*.*

Britain was the world's most efficient producer until the later nineteenth century, when it was overtaken by the USA. During the inter-war years British productivity levels fell further behind the

USA but remained above those prevailing in Europe, and both gaps increased during the second world war. During the long boom almost all OECD countries closed the gap between their productivity levels and those of the USA, but Britain's record seems to have been the least impressive before 1973. Since 1973 Britain's relative position has improved (and the bulk of the improvement surely came after 1979) but the momentum has been lost in the last years of the 1980s.

The convergence hypothesis mentioned above offers a method of interpreting these differences in productivity growth rates. Convergence describes the process by which 'the followers' catch up with the 'lead nation' if they can acquire the 'social capability' to adapt the technology of the leader to their own individual circumstances.[6] Social capability includes the facility to diffuse knowledge; the ability to speed structural change; and the creation of the economic and financial conditions which encourage investment. Convergence theorists argue that after 1945 the conditions for successful catch-up came together – the USA had opened a wide technological gap during wartime; US multinational firms began to establish branch plants throughout the world, taking new ideas with them; the forces of conservatism elsewhere were weakened by war; and freer international trade and payments allowed faster and easier transmission of new ideas. Although convergence theory is not without its problems and critics, it offers a method of approaching Britain's relative decline. Perhaps we should examine Britain's social capability. The best place to conduct such a survey is the performance of British industry since 1945.

*Industrial performance and deindustrialisation.* Economists conventionally divide industry (the production of goods and services for financial gain) into three types: the primary, secondary and tertiary sectors. The primary sector is concerned with growing or extracting natural products and includes agriculture, fishing, forestry and (usually) the mining or extraction of minerals such as oil and coal. The secondary, or *manufacturing*, sector includes those activities which process raw materials into physical goods so that they acquire added value. The tertiary sector embraces all other industries and is concerned with the supply of some form of *service*.

Although the expansion of services has contributed more than any other single sector to the growth of total output in most rich

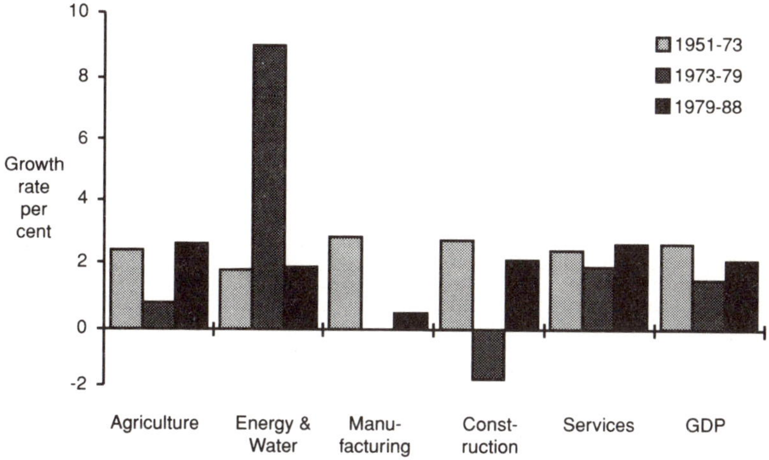


**Figure 1** Rates of growth of output, by sector, 1951–88 (per cent per annum). Note that manufacturing output did not grow at all in the period 1973–79. *Source* C. H. Feinstein and R. C. O. Matthews, 'The growth of output and productivity in the UK: the 1980s as a phase of the post-war period', *National Institute Economic Review*, 1990, p. 81

countries in the twentieth century, the performance of manufacturing has been scrutinised closely because economists tend to see this sector as particularly important. First, productivity growth is more easily achieved in manufacturing than in services. Productivity gains are possible in services, but they may depend upon prior improvements in manufactured goods (as is evident, between the lines, in extract 2.16). Secondly, a much higher proportion of total manufactures is exported than of services. Some services are traded across international frontiers, but the expansion of world trade in manufactures has been the powerhouse of post-war international growth. Finally, many services require low-skilled workers who achieve relatively low levels of productivity. None of these statements is true of all services (see extract 2.16), and the distinction between manufacturing and services has become blurred in recent times (extracts 1.4, 2.15, 2.16), but a strong economy requires a strong manufacturing sector.

In this light, Figure 1 makes rather depressing reading. The manufacturing sector has certainly not led the growth of the British economy in the post-war period. Manufacturing output grew at

***Table 5*** **Comparative rates of growth of labour productivity in manufacturing, 1960–88** (annual percentage growth rates)

| *Country* | *1960–68* | *1968–73* | *1973–79* | *1979–88* |
|---|---|---|---|---|
| France | 6.8 | 5.8 | 2.6 | 2.5 |
| Germany | 4.7 | 4.5 | 2.8 | 1.6 |
| Japan | 9.0 | 10.4 | 4.0 | 3.1 |
| UK | 3.4 | 3.8 | 0.8 | 4.5 |
| USA | 3.2 | 3.8 | 2.1 | 3.7 |

*Sources* G. Meen, 'International comparisons of the UK's long-run economic performance', *Oxford Review of Economic Policy*, 1988, p. xxiii; Feinstein and Matthews, 'The growth of output', p. 88.

about the average rate for all sectors in the long boom, but since then performance has been disappointing, with no growth of output recorded in the 1970s, and only hesitant expansion in the 1980s. The only positive feature of note in Figure 1 is the huge growth of energy output in the 1970s, reflecting the rapid expansion of North Sea gas and oil output. This dramatic growth rate was, however, counterbalanced by contraction in the construction sector and stagnation in manufacturing. There is little compensation in productivity performance. Table 5 compares the growth of labour productivity in manufacturing since 1960 in five countries and shows British performance lagging behind the rest until 1979, since when there have been signs of relative acceleration.

Since 1945 there have been persistent expressions of concern about the performance of parts of British industry. In the 1940s a number of investigations produced a similar catalogue of weaknesses in manufacturing, energy supply and transport: management was weak and had poor technical support; investment levels were low; industrial relations were confrontational; after-sales support and marketing were poor. In sum, significant parts of British industry were ill equipped to deal with a faster pace of technical change. These deficiencies were noted by those nationalising the basic industries, rationalising the long-established consumer goods industries (clothing, textiles, pottery, etc.) and involved in the analyses of many British industries by the Anglo-American Council on Productivity (extract 2.3). These problems did not afflict all British industries (extract 2.4) but signs of stress began to accumulate over the next two decades. British industry lost export markets to competitors in Europe and Japan. World trade in manufactures expanded rapidly during the long boom, but Britain's share

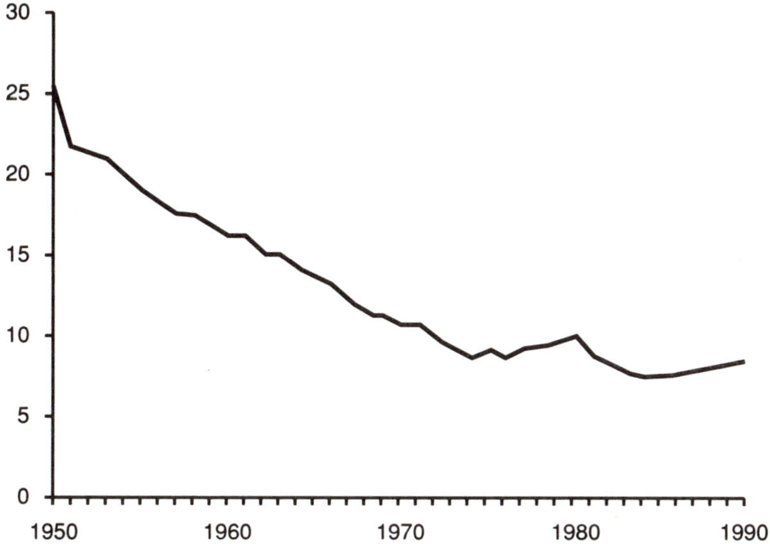


**Figure 2** Britain's share of world trade in manufactures, 1950–90 (per cent). *Sources National Institute Economic Review*, various issues; CSO, *Monthly Digest of Trade Statistics*, various issues

contracted steeply and continuously from 1950 to 1973, as Figure 2 illustrates very clearly.

After the war, Britain's domestic markets were highly protected, but when tariffs began to fall from the late 1950s in the GATT negotiations (see extract 3.4), import penetration began to rise and core parts of British manufacturing – machine tools, shipbuilding and motor car manufacture – began to experience difficulties (extracts 2.5, 2.6, 2.7). It was also becoming obvious that nationalisation had not solved the problems of the energy and transport industries (extract 2.9). Changes in the international economy exacerbated these problems. After 1973 growth rates were lower in all industrial countries, but especially in the UK (Tables 1 and 3 above). Manufacturing employment, which had begun to decline in 1966, fell more rapidly and the sector's share of total output also contracted. Manufacturing output stagnated in the 1970s (Figure 1 and Table 6). Alarm bells began to sound. A new concept, 'deindustrialisation' was added to the economist's lexicon and became a central part of the debates on British economic performance from the late

***Table 6*** **Rates of growth of industrial output, 1951–89** (per cent per annum)

| *Standard Industrial Classification* | *1951–64* | *1964–73* | *1973–79* | *1979–89* |
|---|---|---|---|---|
| Agriculture, forestry, fishing | 2.6 | 2.5 | 0.7 | 2.7 |
| Mining and quarrying | –0.7 | –3.3 | –2.6 | –2.5 |
| Manufacturing | | | | |
| Food, drink, tobacco | 2.6 | 2.7 | 0.7 | 0.7 |
| Chemicals | 5.8 | 6.2 | 2.1 | 2.6 |
| Metals[a] | 2.5 | –0.2 | –3.1 | 0.5 |
| Electrical engineering[b] | 6.0 | 5.7 | 2.0 | 4.8 |
| Mechanical engineering and shipbuilding[c] | 2.4 | 3.2 | –1.3 | –0.7 |
| Vehicles[d] | 4.9 | 0.7 | –2.6 | –0.5 |
| Other metal industries[e] | 2.0 | 0.9 | –1.9 | (f) |
| Textiles[g] | 0.1 | 2.9 | –3.2 | –2.6 |
| Clothing[h] | 2.2 | 1.9 | 0.7 | –0.8 |
| Bricks, pottery, glass, cement[e] | 3.4 | 3.4 | –1.9 | (f) |
| Timber and furniture[e] | 2.2 | 3.5 | –2.5 | (f) |
| Paper, printing, publishing | 4.1 | 2.7 | –0.5 | 1.4 |
| Leather and other manufacturing[h] | 3.2 | 4.5 | 0.8 | 1.5 |
| Total manufacturing | 3.2 | 3.0 | –0.7 | 1.2 |
| Construction | 3.8 | 1.8 | –2.5 | 2.8 |
| Gas, electricity, water | 5.1 | 5.2 | 2.8 | 2.3 |
| Total industrial production[i] | 3.1 | 2.3 | –0.8 | 1.4 |
| Transport | 2.2 | 3.5 | 1.5 | 3.2 |
| Commerce | 3.0 | 3.0 | 1.1 | 5.0 |
| Public and professional services | (1.5) | (2.2) | (2.0) | (0.8) |
| GDP (output based, excludes North Sea output) | 2.8 | 2.7 | 0.5 | 2.3 |
| North Sea oil and gas | | | 181.0 | 1.2 |

*Notes*
(a) 'Iron and steel' up to 1979 and 'Other metals' thereafter.
(b) Contains instrument engineering after 1973.
(c) Mechanical engineering only after 1979. 'Other transport equipment' is excluded from the table (1979-89).
(d) 'Motor vehicles and parts' in 1979–89.
(e) Included in 'Other manufacturing' in 1979–89.
(f) This industry is not recorded separately in the standard industrial classification in use after 1980.
(g) 'Man-made fibres' are separately identified in 1979–89 and have been included in 'Textiles'.
(h) The leather industry is counted in 'Clothing' before 1979 and in 'Other manufacturing' in 1979–89.
(i) As defined before 1973, i.e. mining and quarrying, manufacturing, construction, utilities.

*Sources* Matthews *et al.*, *British Economic Growth*, pp. 228–9, 240–1, CSO, *Blue Book*, various editions.

1970s (extracts 1.4, 1.5, 2.16, 2.17, 3.10). Initially, deindustrialisation appeared to be a uniquely British phenomenon, and the early attempts to explain the process focused exclusively on British conditions.[7] But it soon became clear that other industrial countries were suffering from similar forces, if not to the same extent as the UK, where manufacturing output has been virtually stagnant for twenty years (extract 2.15).

Within this bleak overall picture there have been bright spots. The changes in industrial classification in the post-war years make it impossible to produce consistent and reliable figures of industrial growth for the entire period, but the estimates in Table 6 suggest that within manufacturing food, drink and tobacco, chemicals, electrical engineering and the paper and publishing industries have performed much better than average (see also extracts 2.11, 2.13). There are, moreover, world-class *firms* in many British manufacturing industries, especially those under foreign ownership (extract 2.15). On the other hand, large parts of engineering and the textiles group have been in severe difficulty for a lengthy period. The main criticisms of the weak areas of British manufacturing since 1973 have been remarkably similar to those voiced in the later 1940s. Among what are now called supply-side weaknesses are: the poor quality of British managers, particularly in engineering (extracts 2.6, 2.15, 4.8); low levels of civilian research and development, especially in motor manufacture (extract 2.7); claims that the British financial system has very short-term horizons (extract 5.6); the impact of the system of industrial relations on competitive performance is widely believed to have been harmful (extract 4.6), as have British unions (see below).

Many of the bright spots since 1973 have, however, been outside manufacturing. The most obvious success in the turbulent years of the 1970s was North Sea output, which accounted for a staggering proportion of total production in the period 1979–85 (extract 2.12). But the service sector has also expanded strongly, contributing approximately 54 per cent of national product in 1960 and 70 per cent in 1989. In the mid-1980s sections of British opinion began to proclaim that Britain's manufacturing weaknesses did not matter in the long run; the future lay with services. Within the service sector, there has been substantial growth in financial services (contained within 'Commerce' in Table 6), where productivity levels are high and exports are substantial (extracts 2.14, 2.17). Performance in other parts of the service sector has, however, disappointed. Much was expected of travel and tourism (extract 2.8) but the rosy prospects of the mid-1970s have rather collapsed; foreign tourists have continued to come to the UK and spend money, but the flow in the other direction has increased even more rapidly. The service sector also contains very low productivity activities, with poorly skilled labour, low levels of investment and very limited scope for productivity improvement. Unfortunately, these activities have increased rapidly as the manufacturing sector has stagnated since the early 1970s, with the result that the very large improvements in manufacturing productivity in the 1980s have been muted by comparatively poor productivity performance in services (see the section on the labour market below). The net effect of all this is to suggest that Britain's 'social capability' to absorb and adapt the best practices of the lead nation certainly appear to have been weak in the manufacturing sector in the post-war years and that many of Britain's post-war problems lie in the comparative weakness of significant parts of manufacturing.

*The balance of payments.* The balance of payments is a method of organising transactions between Britain and the rest of the world in so far as they involve payments of foreign currencies or gold. Like any balance sheet, there is a credit and a debit side. The balance of payments is usually divided into three parts:

1. *The balance of trade* – also known as 'visible' trade – actual goods exported and goods imported.

2. *The balance of payments on current account* – includes the balance of trade, that is, imports and exports of goods, plus 'invisible' trade (imports and exports of services – see extract 3.6), plus interest and dividends on investments made by Britons overseas and by foreign nationals in the UK.

3. *The basic balance of payments* – includes the sum of 1 and 2 above plus capital movements and balancing items so that the figure on the debit side is always equal to the figure on the credit side. This item includes total acquisitions and disposals of gold and foreign currencies, with changes in official reserves or liabilities as a balancing item.

Since 1945 countries have managed their balance of payments under two different international financial systems. The first (usually known as the Bretton Woods system) lasted from the 1940s until the early 1970s and obliged all member governments to fix the rate of exchange between their national currency and the dollar. Stable exchange rates should stimulate trade and act as a curb on inflation. However, fixed exchange rate systems or pegged exchange rates cannot easily accommodate the pressure if there are persistently poor and persistently strong economic performers, as the Bretton Woods system found in the early 1970s. It was replaced by a regime of floating currencies, with exchange rates determined by the supply and demand for currencies – at least in theory. Floating exchange rates are particularly attractive during periods of high inflation and should allow governments greater scope than under fixed rates to follow domestic political and economic goals. Most currencies floated during the turbulent years of the 1970s, but the volatility of the 1970s and early 1980s stimulated new attempts to stabilise exchange rates.

In the late 1940s Britain's balance of payments problem was intense. There were huge wartime debts to sterling area countries,* the value of overseas assets had fallen, export capacity was seriously weakened and the need for imports was higher than in 1938 (extract 3.1). Despite rapid recovery in 1946–47, there was no prospect of Britain producing all the industrial goods and foodstuffs she needed (extracts 1.1 and 2.2). The only reliable source of essential imports was the dollar area (the USA and Canada) but Britain lacked dollars. A big loan from the USA and Canada in 1945 and US Marshall aid to Britain and the rest of Europe after 1947 eased the problem, but policy discussions were dominated by the dollar shortage until the mid-1950s. Britain adjusted to dollar shortages faster than other European countries (extract 3.2) but a general devaluation of most currencies, including sterling, against the dollar in 1949 and further recovery of European production was needed to ease the position. By the early 1950s Britain's current account began to look healthier.

Figure 3 shows the size of the current balance (after all transactions involving oil have been removed) as a proportion of national product, with surpluses above the central axis and deficits below. The non-oil current balance was pretty strong in the 1950s, with no deficits, apart from 1951, when the Korean war complicated the picture. But balance of payments problems re-emerged at mid-decade. Britain's reserves of foreign currency seemed to foreigners inadequate to cover overseas debts and confidence crises were regular (extract 3.3). Britain was also losing its share of world

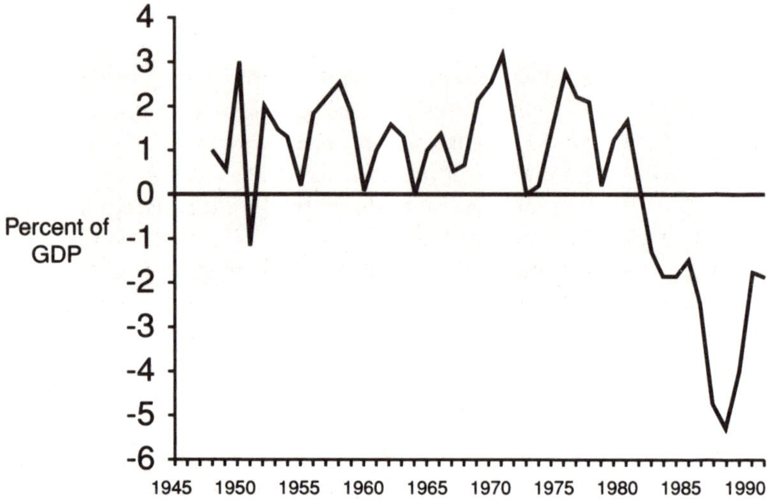


**Figure 3** Britain's non-oil current account, 1948–92 (current balance as a percentage of GDP). *Sources Annual Abstract of Statistics*, various editions; *Economic Trends*, annual supplement, 1993

manufactured trade at an alarming rate in the 1950s and more substantial problems were developing. In the 1960s import penetration of the domestic market, though limited, began to accelerate as tariff reductions under GATT began to gather momentum (extract 3.4). Although the non-oil current account was reasonably strong in the 1960s, it was not strong enough in the face of reserves which were still too low and international debts which were deemed too high. A series of balance of payments crises in the 1960s culminated in devaluation in 1967 (extract 3.5). Unfortunately, Britain devalued when the Bretton Woods system was becoming increasingly unstable and, though devaluation did bring about a big improvement in the current account in the early 1970s, the instability in international finance, the rise of inflationary forces in the British economy and the growing belief that Britain's rate of economic growth would be faster if fixed exchange rates were abandoned led to the decision to float sterling in 1972 (extract 3.8).

During the 1950s and 1960s substantial changes occurred in the pattern of British trade, with a switch from the slowly growing markets of the Commonwealth to more rapidly growing but fiercely competitive markets of Europe (Figure 4). The culmination of this

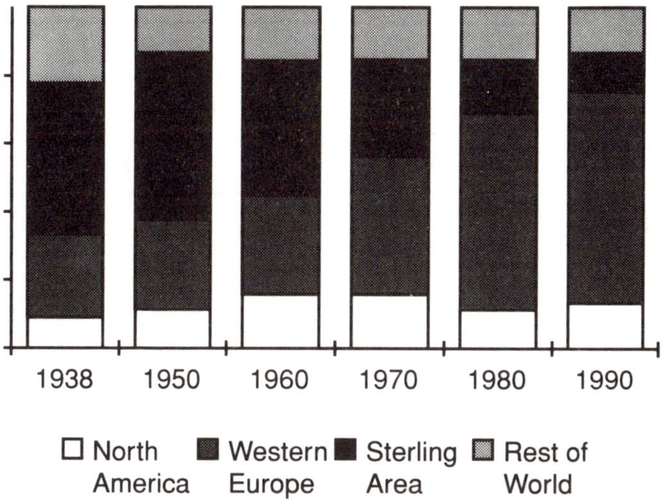


**Figure 4** The geographical distribution of British exports since 1938.
*Source Annual Abstract of Statistics*, various issues

shift was Britain's entry into the EEC in 1973. At the time, Britain's entry was seen as an opportunity for exporters (extract 3.8) but EEC entry involved a phased abolition of trade barriers with European competitors and import penetration appears to have accelerated.

Although floating exchange rates, which Britain adopted in 1972, in theory allow policy-makers greater freedom to pursue domestic goals, in practice British governments found that floating exchange rates were subject to large, unpredictable movements and that domestic policies had to be conducted in ways which won the confidence of the foreign exchange markets. The classic illustration came in 1976, when the markets lost confidence in the policies pursued by the Labour government, which was forced to borrow from the International Monetary Fund in order to restore order to the markets (extract 3.9). However, the new market confidence in sterling was a very mixed blessing. It coincided with rising North Sea production at a time when oil prices were high and unstable. The value of sterling began a long rise from 1977 to 1981. The rising exchange rate imposed severe competitive difficulties on British industry, whether manufacturing or services, home- or export-oriented (Figure 5 and extract 2.10). Manufacturing was hit very hard, output fell by one-fifth between 1979 and 1982, so that when

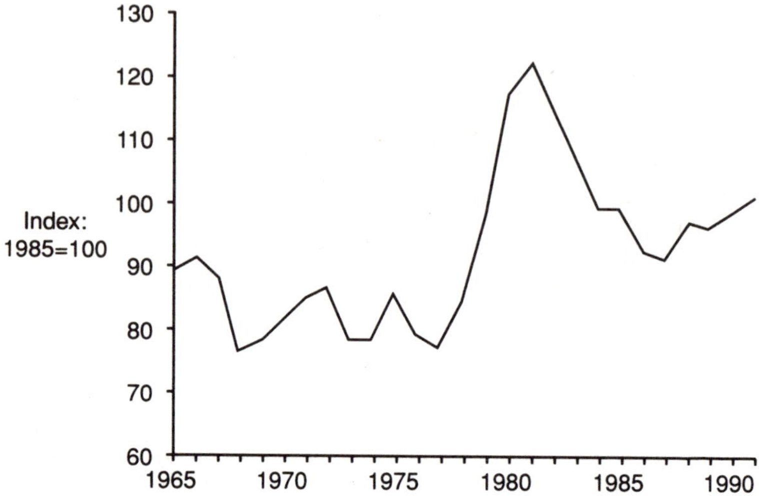


**Figure 5** The competitiveness of British manufacturing, 1965–91. Figures of normalised relative unit labour costs, weighted using 1985 levels of competitiveness as a base. Upward movement indicates a loss of competitiveness, so the rise from 1976 to 1981 indicates a massive handicap for exporters. For further details on how to interpret the data see extract 2.10. *Source Economic Trends*, annual supplement, 1994, table 1.20

markets began to recover in 1982 domestic suppliers were unable to meet the demand. For the first time in more than three centuries, Britain became a net importer of manufactures during the 1980s and the non-oil current account went into severe deficit (extract 3.10, Figure 6).

The current account deficit was closed by oil exports, but severe damage had been done to Britain's manufacturing export capacity (Figures 3 and 6). Governments were not prepared to abandon floating exchange rates. Sterling was now a petro-currency* at a time of great instability in petroleum prices. By 1987, however, there was renewed British interest in pegging the exchange rate both as a sign of commitment to membership of the European Union and as a new weapon against inflation, which began to rise alarmingly in the late 1980s. Accordingly, Britain joined the Exchange Rate Mechanism of the European Monetary System in October 1990, but the experiment was not a success and ended in abject failure after less than two years (extract 3.11).

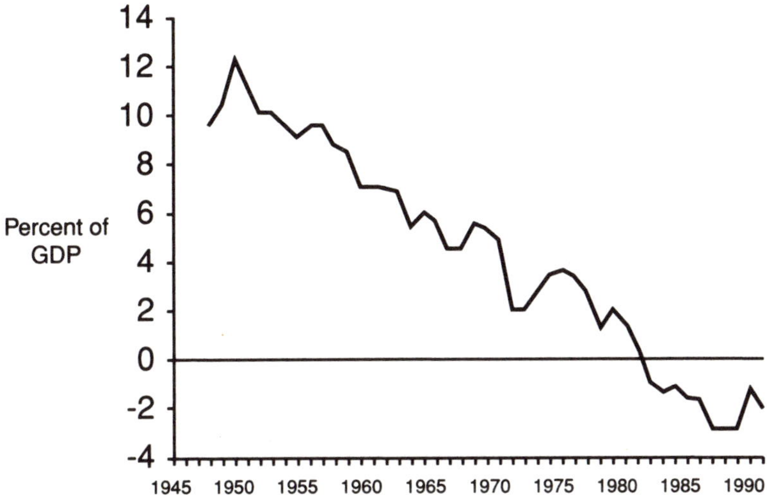


**Figure 6** Britain's balance of trade in manufactures, 1948–92 (as a percentage of GDP). *Sources Annual Abstract of Statistics*, various editions; *Economic Trends*, annual supplement, 1993

The balance of payments has been a recurrent problem throughout the post-war period. Whereas the growth of trade has been a stimulus to the faster growth enjoyed by Japan and many European countries, weakness in the balance of payments has frequently caused the British government to sacrifice its growth target. The efforts of Keynesian economists to argue that the balance of payments has constrained the British growth rate have, however, been largely unconvincing (see below). It is more likely that the weaknesses already noted in some British manufacturing firms have resulted not only in slow growth for much of the post-war period but also in weak competitive performance. The steady collapse of the manufacturing trade balance noted in Figure 6 has been counterbalanced by better, but by no means outstanding, performance in world trade in services and the exports of North Sea oil and gas (extracts 3.6 and 2.12). The real problem for the balance of payments in the 1990s is what happens when the oil runs out.

*The labour market.* During the post-war period there have been important developments in employment, unemployment and the industrial relations system. In addition to the rising numbers at work and reductions in the length of the working week already

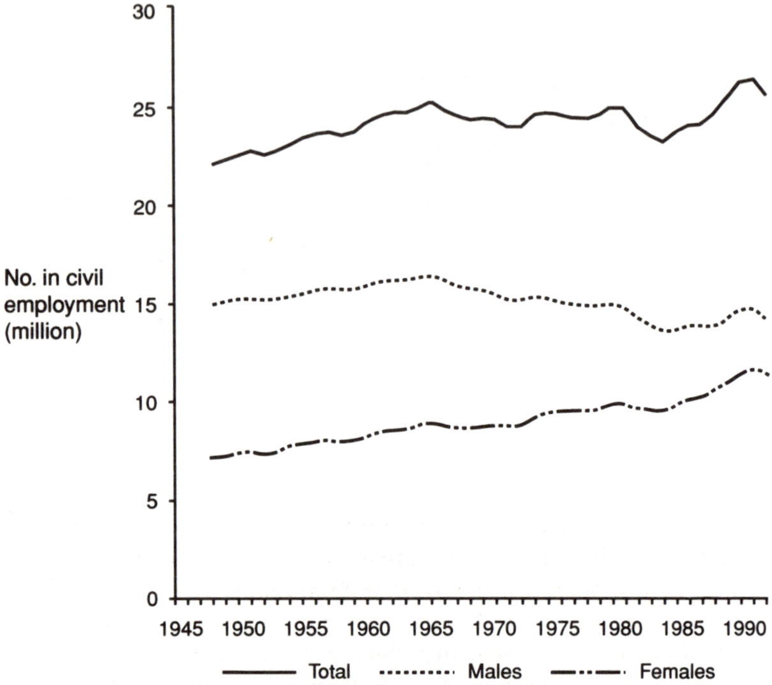


**Figure 7** Changes in civilian employment, 1948–91 (million workers). *Source Annual Abstract of Statistics*, various issues

noted, there have been significant shifts in the gender composition of employment (Figure 7 and extract 4.7). The number of male employees has changed very little in the post-war period, but there has been a steady rise in the number of female workers, so that in the 1990s they comprise approximately 40 per cent of the civilian work force. A large proportion of women workers are employed on a part-time basis, rising from a quarter of the female work force in the early 1960s to just under half in the 1980s and 1990s. Driving these changes have been the relative decline of manufacturing production and the rise of the service sector, discussed in the previous sections, and advantages to employers, particularly in services, in employing workers on part-time contracts. Accompanying the changes in the gender composition of the work force have been significant shifts in the sectoral distribution, as can be seen in Table 7.

*Table 7* **Proportion of the British work force employed in different sectors, 1931–91** (per cent)

| *Year* | *Primary*[a] | *Production*[b] | *Services* | *Not known* |
|---|---|---|---|---|
| 1931 | 11.9 | 37.0 | 50.6 | 0.5 |
| 1951 | 8.9 | 43.6 | 47.4 | 0.1 |
| 1961 | 6.6 | 44.3 | 48.7 | 0.4 |
| 1971 | 4.3 | 42.9 | 52.8 | – |
| 1981 | 3.2 | 35.3 | 61.5 | – |
| 1991 | 1.9 | 26.9 | 71.2 | – |

*Notes*

(a) Before 1975 agriculture, forestry, fishing and mining and quarrying; after 1975 agriculture, forestry, fishing and coal, oil and natural gas extraction and processing.

(b) Manufacturing; gas, water, electricity; construction.

*Source Annual Abstract of Statistics*, various issues.

The corollary of these changes in the pattern of distribution of employment and the relative performance of manufacturing and services has been significant changes in the unemployment rate. During the war there was a strong politial and ethical commitment to the maintenance of full employment in peacetime (extract 4.1) and the first three post-war decades were marked by unprecedentedly low levels of unemployment. Full employment probably owed much more to the working out of real economic forces (the rise in investment in the post-war period and fast growth of world trade and incomes) than to government policy, but businesses, unions and politicians acted as if government had the power to determine the level of unemployment. After the mid-1970s, however, unemployment began to climb and the recessions of both the early 1980s and the early 1990s were accompanied by severe rises in unemployment. The concept of 'full employment' disappeared in the 1980s. A series of highly controversial changes in official statistics in the 1980s make it impossible to give a consistent picture of the changing pattern of unemployment in the whole post-war period, but Figure 8 shows changes in the rate on both the old basis of calculation and the basis which had been established by 1989. The rises after the mid-1970s are clearly discernible, as is the impact of the new method of counting unemployment.

Despite these enormous changes in labour market conditions during the post-war period, there have been remarkable continuities in the criticisms of the way that that market has functioned. For

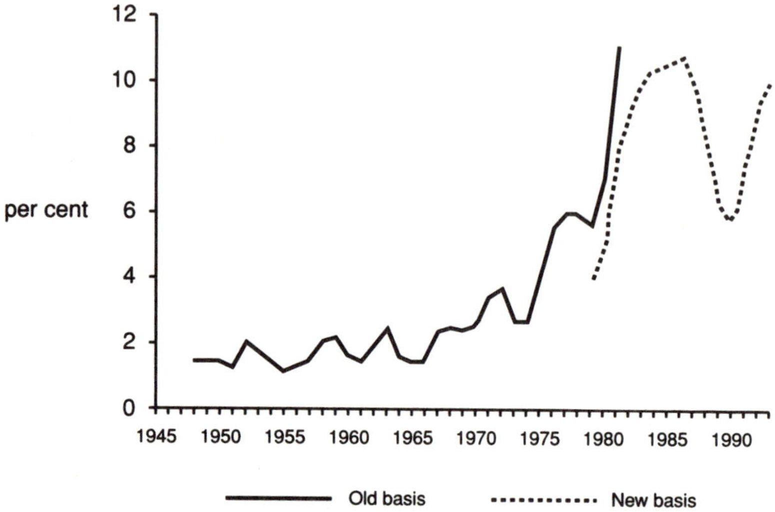


**Figure 8** The rate of unemployment in the UK, 1945–93 (annual averages, per cent). *Sources Annual Abstract of Statistics*, various issues; *Employment Gazette*, historical supplement, April 1989

much of the post-war period, commentators have readily identified trade union behaviour as a principal cause of problems in both the labour market and the wider economy. Inflation has been a constant worry and union responsibility for rising wages and prices has been accepted almost without question. From 1947 to 1979 there were regular attempts to commit unions to wage restraint (extract 4.2). It was also widely believed that labour market power gave unions the ability to obstruct technical change, impose over-generous manning levels, maintain shortages of skilled workers and technicians (extract 4.5), resist pressure to work harder and disrupt production through strikes (extracts 4.6, 5.9, 5.10). Labour market power also gave union leaders a seat at the table in the making of national economic policy (extract 4.4). This combination of strong shop-floor trade unionism and tripartite policy-making (by leaders of government, industry and unions) had been successful and popular during wartime, but as evidence of Britain's relatively high inflation and slow growth began to accumulate from the late 1950s, trade union influence over policy was seen as harmful, leading to policies which fortified union power on the shop floor but only exacerbated the causes of high inflation and slow growth. Power is

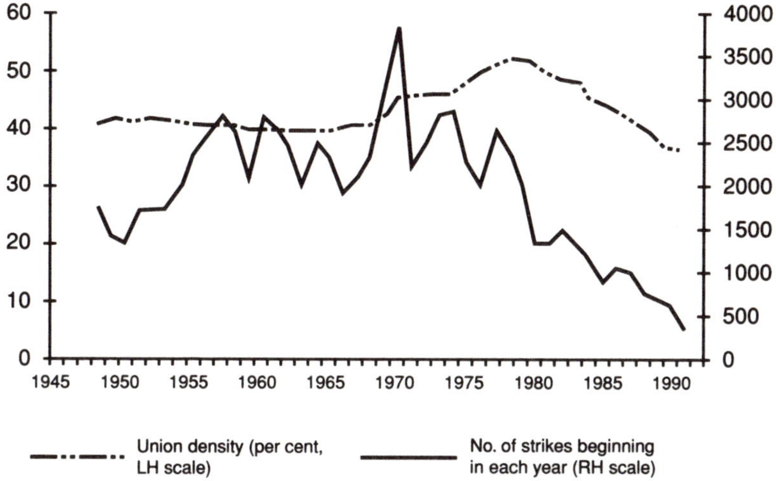


**Figure 9** Changes in union density and strike activity, 1947–92. Union density is the proportion of those in civilian employment who are members of trade unions. *Sources* Department of Employment, *British Labour Statistics, 1886–1968*; *Annual Abstract of Statistics*, various editions

impossible to measure objectively but trade union strength clearly derived from the ability of unions to recruit workers through devices such as the closed shop, especially in manufacturing industries. Figure 9 shows changes in union density (the proportion of those in employment belonging to unions) and the number of strikes during the post-war years. The most significant aspect of Figure 9 is the rise in union density during the 1970s when British economic performance deteriorated so badly.

Union leaders did not share this view of organised labour as a threat to economic progress. Although there were celebrated cases of union resistance to change (the docks, shipbuilding, newspaper publishing), most unions saw themselves as fighting for a share in the fruits of economic progress (extracts 4.3). After 1965, however, governments gave much higher priority to trade union reform. An authoritative royal commission under Lord Donovan investigated British industrial relations and found the cause of labour market problems in the way collective bargaining institutions had evolved (extract 4.6). Successive governments blamed the unions alone and sought to weaken their powers. Reforms proposed by both the

Wilson and the Heath governments either came to naught or were blunted by union resistance, and the 'union problem' assumed even greater proportions. While in opposition in the later 1970s the Conservatives planned to make taming the unions a policy priority (extract 5.9) and the Thatcher government expelled the unions from policy-making circles, passed a string of anti-union Acts and did nothing to mitigate the effects of rapidly rising unemployment in the early 1980s. Unions were certainly weakened, the number of strikes continued to fall (Figure 8) and the government skilfully turned much of the blame for both the mass unemployment of the 1980s and relatively slow growth before 1979 on to the unions (extract 4.9). The government's analysis was given greater force by signs which began to emerge during the mid-1980s of a 'productivity miracle' in manufacturing during the early 1980s. There was good evidence that productivity growth in manufacturing in the 1980s was fastest where unions had been strongest in 1979 and where the forces of depression from 1979 to 1982 had been most severe. Elaborate theories were constructed which supported the view of the government's analysis: relatively slow growth before 1979 had been the result of weak competition which allowed employers to make mistakes without having to face bankruptcy and had given unions scope to insist on overmanning, slowly changing production methods and excessive wage rises (extract 5.10). However, this analysis and much of the 'productivity miracle' literature[8] appears somewhat premature. Even more recent assessments of labour market performance during the 1980s has suggested that the 'humbling' of the trade unions has not made wages more flexible or more responsive to changing unemployment, nor is there any evidence of a sustained rise in the rate of productivity growth in the economy as a whole (extract 4.10). Perhaps the unions have been more sinned against than sinning after all.

## The historiography of the 'British disease'

Taking Tables 1 and 2 together, the British economy has followed a disappointing path of steady, unspectacular progress since 1951, with no economic miracles but no great collapses either. Popular perceptions have, however, been far more volatile. Complacency was rife until the mid–1950s. British policy-makers viewed the

French and German economies as weak links in European recovery and potential supplicants for aid from Britain (extract 3.2). By the 1980s, on the other hand, Correlli Barnett's overblown picture of 'the dank reality of [Britain's] segregated, subliterate, unskilled, unhealthy and institutionalised proletariat hanging on the nipple of state maternalism' (extract 5.7) was widely accepted as a faithful picture of the state of the nation. Neither account comes close to being a balanced assessment. Excessive optimism and pessimism have, however, coloured the historiography of Britain's post-war economic performance.

*Accounts from within the consensus.* The 'British disease' has been diagnosed by economists, sociologists, political scientists, anthropologists, industrialists, bankers, politicians, administrators and every type of committee. Economic historians began to study the post-war period systematically in the 1960s (led, interestingly enough, by the foray of the renowned medievalist, Professor M. M. Postan, into post-war European economic development[9]) and have been coming to terms with this wide-ranging literature ever since. Naturally enough, the debates within economics over the nature and causes of the growth process have done most to shape economic historians' perspectives on relative decline, especially as the demarcation line between economic history and applied economics has become very blurred. But economics and economic history have also been profoundly influenced by wider ideas on 'political economy' which embrace the political, ideological and social dimensions. Accordingly, the historiography of the 'British disease' has been classified in relation to a broad consensus on the way the economy, economic policy and the political system worked in the first three post-war decades. 'Consensus' is a notoriously difficult word for historians but it is used here in a loose sense to embrace the climate of ideas about economic policy and performance which is sometimes termed the 'Keynesian era'. It includes 'collectivist politics', comprising the welfare state, the mixed economy, interventionist economic management, the incorporation of producer interest groups (the employers' associations and the TUC) into policy-making and a foreign economic policy centring on the 'special relationship' with the USA and Britain's view of itself as a world power. The whole edifice received intellectual support from Keynesian economic analysis which held that the free enterprise economy was inherently unstable.

Keynesians tended to concentrate on changes in the main macroeconomic* variables (aggregate national income, total consumption, saving, government expenditure and the foreign balance) which Keynes had used in constructing his *General Theory*. They saw Britain's comparatively low level of investment, weakness in the balance of payments, and the quality of macroeconomic policy-making as the keys to understanding slow growth. The initial culprit was the 'stop-go' pattern of British growth. In the late 1950s, governments began to experience difficulties in achieving simultaneously their goals of full employment, stable prices and external stability. Policy appeared to be driven by short-term considerations (the level of unemployment, the state of the balance of payments) and insufficient attention was paid, or so it was believed, to the creation of conditions conducive to rising industrial investment. The sources of 'stop-go' were found in inadequate official statistics (extract 5.1), insufficient policy instruments and Britain's 'balance of payments constraint'. If official statistics were produced too slowly, government could easily so mistime its policy intervention that it contracted a downswing or boosted an upswing of the trade cycle. These arguments led to the hypothesis that policy 'destabilised' the economy, with adverse effects on long-term growth.[10] As policy-makers in the mid–1950s found it more difficult to achieve all their goals simultaneously, they looked for a wider range of policies – incomes policies to curb inflation, tax incentives to boost investment, 'planning' to accelerate the growth rate (extracts 5.2 and 5.3). Underlying all this effort was concern about the balance of payments. The cause of the 'stop' phase was invariably weakness in the balance of payments. Keynesian economists elaborated theories which made the growth rate a function of trade performance. The most persuasive concentrated on the difference between, on the one hand, the amount of additional British exports which will flow from a given rise in world incomes and, on the other, the amount of additional imports flowing into Britain from the same rise in British incomes.[11] It is easy to maintain fixed exchange rates, as under the Bretton Woods system, if these *income elasticities of demand* are similar. Initial calculations seemed to show, however, that Britain had very unfavourable elasticities – if British and world incomes grew at the same rate, Britain would experience a balance of payments problem because domestic demand for imported goods would have grown much faster than world demand for British exports. The implication was that the British economy had to grow slowly because of the relative unwillingness of the rest of the world to take British exports.

Economic historians writing in the 1960s embraced much, but certainly not all, of this approach. Postan, for example, had few doubts that interventionist, discriminatory economic policies were a necessity for faster growth. Sidney Pollard, who published the first textbook to cover the post-war British economy, emphasised the role of investment in the growth process and explained Britain's poor investment record largely in terms of mistaken macroeconomic policies.[12] But neither Postan nor Pollard presented a simple Keynesian account of post-war British economic development. Postan emphasised the importance of institutions in explaining why national growth rates differed. Pollard, on the other hand, was very sensitive to the growing signs of microeconomic* weaknesses in the 1950s. He was one of the first to note that the calculations of the elasticities of demand took no account of non-price factors, and that if British firms had been able to make motor cars and other consumer durable goods of similar quality to the Germans and Japanese, British elasticities would have been more favourable. These were among the first indications of the importance of the supply side in the British disease.

*The growing evidence of microeconomic failure and the power of institutions.* The growing evidence of microeconomic failure in the 1960s has been a strong theme of previous sections. Economists' interest in supply-side problems began to revive, especially after the discovery of the importance of non-price factors in Britain's competitive weakness. Reinforcing the importance of the supply side were the first applications of growth accounting and the accumulating volume of studies of post-war industry by industrial economists and economic historians which had identified weaknesses in management, labour, industrial relations, research activity and product innovation by British firms.[13] But this merely posed the question: what caused the supply-side weaknesses?

The answer has been found in the existence of institutions. An indigenous British institutional approach has long flourished within economic history, industrial relations and sociology and has occasionally flowered within economics. The most prominent early institutional explanations of Britain's relative decline identified cultural conservatism, especially among elite groups. Balogh's account (extract 5.4), for example, blamed the rules of selection and training of civil servants as the principal causes of inadequate economic policies since 1945. More ambitiously, G. C. Allen identified a more pervasive cultural conservatism, emanating from upper middle-class disdain for industry and transmitted more broadly by the education system, which produced 'cultivated citizens' but shunned vocational training for industry. At the same time, twentieth-century industrial relations were profoundly coloured by conflictual attitudes which had their roots in the industrial revolution (extract 5.5). At a more prosaic level, there have been frequent complaints that the British financial system is not geared to the needs of industry (extract 5.6) because it is dominated by the City of London, with its traditional interests in international finance and trade. Together these arguments pointed to the enormous power of institutions developed in the nineteenth century or earlier over twentieth-century actions, decisions and behaviour.

This British institutional tradition has tended to be historical and descriptive but the institutional approach has been enriched in more recent years by a more analytical approach, derived initially from the work of an American economist, Mancur Olson, who has formulated a simple but compelling method. He argues that the pace and pattern of economic growth are affected by the number, type and longevity of *collective interest groups* in each developed economy.[14] Broadly speaking, the longer a nation enjoys political and social stability, the more collective interest groups it is likely to have, and the slower its rate of growth is likely to be. A second study of the impact of institutions on British economic development, also led by American scholars, has focused attention on the slow development in Britain of the intensively managed giant corporation pioneered in the USA at the turn of the present century.[15] Long-run historical and institutional forces prevented the adoption of US management techniques in Britain and explain Britain's comparative failure in manufacturing.

Initially, this new analytical concern with the long term and the supply side was absorbed into the consensus approach. Politicians, for example, called for 'modernisation' of British institutions to provide a better, firmer foundation for tackling the problems of low investment and balance of payments weakness (extract 5.3). But changes taking place in British economic policy, in the performance of the British economy and in the more ethereal world of economic theory combined to shift the focus of blame for Britain's relative decline. The Wilson government's failure to secure faster growth encouraged a search for new, non-consensual policies. The emergence of 'stagflation'* presented Keynesian theory with economic conditions which it found difficult to comprehend and sharpened political conflicts which hastened the decline of consensus. Class-based analyses of Britain's economic problems were developed in this new climate (extract 5.8) but the new political and economic conditions fostered above all the rise of monetarist and new classical ideas.

*Anti-consensus accounts and the power of institutions.* In the 1970s the economics profession broke into open dispute about how the economy worked. From the University of Chicago, Milton Friedman claimed to have an analytical system which was more capable than Keynesian ideas of understanding the causes of stagflation and the more turbulent economic conditions of the 1970s. Friedman's doctrine has become known as monetarism, but this is an oversimplification both of Friedman's own work and of the direction which his followers have subsequently taken. His analysis combined a new macroeconomic approach which, in very broad terms, said that governments could hope to control inflation rather than unemployment and growth, and a microeconomic dimension which, again in very broad terms, insisted that government intervention would be harmful to the pattern and pace of economic development – governments should withdraw from the economy and leave to market forces decisions about the allocation of resources, the determination of prices and other fundamental matters. After a period of great turbulence in economic theory, this approach and refinements of it triumphed. Economists now argue that the policy regime pursued since 1945 has been part of the problem rather than of the solution.

These currents in intellectual ideas were reinforced by what was happening in the British economy in the 1970s. There was a growing sense that the inflationary 'wage-price' spiral had been underwritten by governments and increasing ambivalence towards the institutions upon which the consensus had been built. The nationalised industries, for example, had been immensely popular in the 1940s, but by the 1970s they were perceived as inefficient, poorly managed and a millstone around the necks of taxpayers (extracts 2.9 and 5.10). There was also growing resentment about the tax levels which were thought to be necessary to support the cost of welfare and public sector inefficiency. Above all, interventionist policies appeared to give too much power to the trade unions.

In the political sphere, the combination of radical new ideas on the role of the state and growing discontent with many aspects of economic policy created the conditions for Thatcherism. But the new climate also helped to shape the historiography of Britain's relative decline. Sir Keith Joseph, probably the most important advocate of new classical economic and political ideas in Britain, demonstrated the potential of the new situation (extract 5.9). Even in this brief passage, the anti-interventionist and monetarist foundations of his approach are very clear and in the second paragraph he hits all the targets of growing public disenchantment – inflation, the public sector and the trade unions. Previous 'consensual' policies are presented as a 'prison', leading to the 'slow disintegration' of the nation state. It would be unwise to dismiss this as merely party political propaganda. In the later 1970s important studies of British (un)competitiveness identified trade unions as a significant cause of inefficiency.[16] There was strong and growing intellectual support for anti-consensual views.

The most important contribution to this anti-consensus view, but from a very different political perspective, has been Correlli Barnett's *The Audit of War* (extract 5.7). Barnett, too, identifies the roots of the British disease in poor industrial leadership, confrontational industrial relations and worker resistance to change which had their roots deep in Britain's industrial revolution. But he also demonstrates from government records that these weaknesses were recognised during the second world war and that, even during the most critical phases of the Battles of Britain and the Atlantic, almost nothing was done to remedy the faults. Even in a national emergency both sides of manufacturing industry preferred to fight the class enemy rather than the Axis powers. This is not a recognition of the power of institutions so much as an indictment of the British political establishment for failing to tackle the problem after the war. Barnett is an advocate of 'Prussian-style' state-directed industrial modernisation and he criticises the 'liberal establishment' for undertaking the 'social revolution' of the welfare state rather than the 'economic revolution' of industrial reorganisation when peace returned. Moreover, without efficient manufacturing industries, the New Jerusalem was impossible to sustain in the longer term.

This is a highly controversial thesis which has provoked enthusiastic reviews and intensely critical comment in equal measure. As a document in the evolving interpretation of the British disease it is, however, vitally important. Barnett has skilfully acknowledged the importance of long-run, institutional weaknesses in relative decline, but has marked the imbalance of policy (favouring social consensus rather than industrial growth) since 1945 as the key to the acceleration of relative decline. Barnett's approach seems, for example, to have penetrated the thinking of Nick Crafts, the leading academic interpreter of British economic performance (extract 5.10). He divides the causes of relative decline between those resulting from long-term weaknesses (inadequate investment in plant, machinery and the work force skills needed to exploit new technologies fully) and those caused by the weak competitive environment (the 'soft budgets' of firms) fostered by cosy collusion between leaders of government, business and trade unions between 1945 and 1979.

Although Crafts does not attempt to measure the relative significance of long-run institutional weaknesses and post-war collusion, he clearly expects very significant improvement in the growth rate from the changes in 'policy configuration' after 1979. In the new economic environment, employers are burdened by intense competition, unions by mass unemployment and the government is committed to cultivating enterprise and allowing inefficient firms to go bust. The argument is interesting but the evidence upon which it is based is hardly compelling. The argument that firms' budgets were soft before 1979 hardly squares with the lost export markets and rising import penetration noted above. The collapse of the cotton textile, shipbuilding, motor cycle and machine tool industries came well before 1979. The fast growth of the French and German economies between 1950 and 1973 was fostered by soft budgets, which in the French case were deliberately created by government.[17] More interestingly, this revisionist view of post-war policies as a powerful cause of continuing relative decline rests upon a tiny empirical base. To carry conviction, the 'new revisionism' needs an improvement of Britain's relative performance after 1979. It is surprising just how weak that evidence is. The figures show that the growth rate improves after 1979 (Table 2), but growth was especially slow in the 1970s and the estimates of national product are undoubtedly less reliable after 1979 than before. Productivity performance was especially strong in manufacturing during the 1980s

(Table 5), but this was achieved with output which has barely grown for two decades (Figure 1, extract 2.16). Productivity growth in the whole economy during the 1980s is nothing special.[18] The case for a significant improvement in performance rests ultimately on the evidence of the closing of the efficiency gap with the USA and Europe between 1979 and 1990. No comparative figures of productivity levels are yet available for 1990 and Britain's relative position was slipping at the end of the 1980s (Table 4). This is scarcely compelling evidence, especially if the arguments about firms' 'soft budgets' before 1979 are as devoid of content as is suggested above. The debate about the causes of the British disease will surely continue.

# 1
# Aggregate economic performance

The main weakness of the British economy has been the tendency for growth to be slower than in comparable economies. This problem did not, however, become fully apparent until the 1960s and, even then, slow growth tended to be only one problem among many. In the immediate post-war period the main concern was to return the economic system to 'normalcy', and the re-establishment of peacetime patterns of supply and demand. Thereafter there has been a strong tendency for inflation and the balance of payments to deteriorate whenever the economy has shown any sign of acceleration in the rate of growth.

## 1.1 The progress towards normalcy by December 1946

The switch from wartime to peacetime patterns of supply and demand was rapid and involved enormous structural changes in the economy. At the beginning of 1947 there was satisfaction at what had been achieved but concern that reconstruction was only partially complete.

At the end of the war 42 per cent of the nation's manpower was in the armed forces or was directly engaged in supplying them. Only 2 per cent were producing exports and less than 8 per cent were providing and maintaining the nation's capital equipment. The nation's main task was to demobilise this war structure and to set the civilian economy moving.

This has been done with very little dislocation. By the end of 1946, ... the proportion of the nation's manpower in the armed forces or directly engaged in supplying them had fallen from 42 per cent to less than 10 per cent. In this process the number of unemployed in Britain has never exceeded 400,000 or 2 per cent of the insured population ...

The number [of workers] in manufacturing industry and building is somewhat larger than it was before the war, but within this field there has been a very considerable switch from the textile and clothing industries to the metal and engineering industries; there is substantially more employment in agriculture, public utilities and transport, but less in mining. The increase in the total employed population and much of the additional manpower made available by a considerable reduction in distribution and other consumers' services has been absorbed by the increase of the defence and public services ...

By the end of [1946] the rate of national output was probably not significantly below pre-war over the economy as a whole ... and has given us a start with each of the tasks of reconstruction of the British economy – exports, industrial re-equipment, repair of war damage, housing, and an increased flow of consumer goods ...

The expansion of production and consumption throughout 1946 put a heavy strain in particular upon coal and power supplies, but also upon steel, transport and other basic industries and services. Coal production in the year as a whole exceeded the production of 1945 by 3.6 per cent. But it did not grow nearly fast enough to match the growing consumption as the conversion of industry and the restoration of the civil economy got under way. The by no means unfavourable industrial results for 1946 were achieved only by a draft of 5 million tons on coal stocks. In a sense, indeed, we have been living on a coal overdraft. The demand for power likewise exceeded the capacity of the power stations; the demand for transport was up to the limit of what could be carried by the railways' depleted rolling stock; the demand for steel was more than could be produced or imported. Indeed, our basic industries and services were limiting the nation's productive effort ...

The central fact of 1947 is that we have not enough resources to do all that we want to do. We have barely enough to do all that we *must* do. Whether we reckon in terms of manpower, coal, electricity, steel or national production as a whole, the conclusion is unavoidable. To get all we want, production would have to be increased by at least 25 per cent. This is clearly impossible in 1947.

There is no reason for surprise about this. We have come through six years of all-out effort. We lost less men than some of our allies;

we were saved from enemy occupation. But our losses, though less obvious, are very real and are now making themselves felt – first in our import-export problem and, second, in the need for rebuilding our basic industries. We must find means to pay for imports which we formerly got in return for our overseas investments,[1] and we must make up six years' arrears of industrial re-equipment. These are basic things, and to put them right is a huge job of work – especially as we must at the same time rebuild our battered housing, restore our depleted flocks and herds and produce more clothing and household goods.

*Economic Survey for 1947*, London, 1947, pp. 9–11, 16.

## 1.2 Slow growth in the 1950s

Since 1960 the Organisation for Economic Co-operation and Development has published annual economic surveys of its members, who constitute the world's rich industrial economies. Britain's performance was relatively poor when measured against the other members of the club, especially during the 1950s, as this survey makes clear.

The failure of the economy to sustain any prolonged period of growth of output during the 1950s and the slow growth of productivity, both actual and potential, compare unfavourably with the record of industrialised industries on the continent ...

The rate of growth of GNP in the UK in the 1950s was about half the rate achieved in the member countries of the EEC; the relation of the UK and EEC growth rates did not change between the two five year periods[2] despite the fact that, by 1955, the reconstruction phase, which might have been expected to favour a faster rate of growth on the continent was practically over. When allowance has been made for the fact that ... employment was growing more slowly in the UK than was general on the continent, the comparison is still unfavourable; the growth of GNP per head of employed population was 2.5 to 3 times faster on the continent up to 1955 and twice as fast subsequently. Output per man-hour in industry shows a similar comparison; the increase in the UK was between one-half and one-third of that in the EEC countries.

The slow rate of growth of output and productivity in the last decade was not accompanied by price stability ... [T]he rise in British prices was substantial and rather greater than that in the EEC countries other than France, which had to make two devaluations during this period.

But it is when trends in the external balance are considered that the comparison with the continental countries becomes particularly striking. The elasticity of demand for imports[3] does not seem to have been substantially different in the UK and in the EEC countries. But the development of exports shows a very strong contrast. After an insignificant rise in the first half of the decade, UK exports rose only half as fast as imports between 1955 and 1960. In the EEC countries, on the other hand, exports and imports grew in parallel during the 1955–60 period and in the first half of the decade exports had been rising substantially faster than imports. Even allowing for the progressive improvement in the terms of trade[4] in this period, the slow growth of exports stands out as one of the most striking features of the performance of the UK economy in the 1950s. As a result, the trade balance deteriorated by about $0.8 billion in the first half of the 1950s and improved only slightly in the second half, whereas the trade balance of the EEC countries improved by $1.4 billion and $1.5 billion in the same periods. Over the whole decade, the UK's gold and foreign exchange reserves rose by $0.4 billion, whilst those of the EEC countries rose by $11.0 billion.

*Obstacles to growth in the 1950s*

The problems underlying the UK's relatively low rate of growth in the 1950s are complex and, to some extent, interlocking. They are unlikely to respond to any single, simple solution, but certain factors with important implications for policy may be singled out from the experience of the past decade.

The low rate of growth cannot be ascribed to any inadequacy of overall demand. The problem lay rather in the fact that, in contrast to what was happening in many continental countries, exports did not play a major dynamic role in the growth process. It was home demand, in the case of the UK, that spearheaded development over the 1950s, and through successive cycles this led, after a relatively short time, to a deterioration in the balance of payments accompanied by internal strains, particularly on the labour market. The picture was, repeatedly, one of home demand rising faster than output, with exports insufficiently dynamic to look after the balance of payments, and the authorities [were] required to impose frequent measures of restraint. The external payments position was further complicated by the relatively large burden of defence expenditure overseas and, later, of overseas aid.

A faster rise of exports would have been difficult to achieve given the trend of costs and prices. A striking phenomenon during much of the period was the fact that, in the UK, rising money incomes were associated with price increases to a significantly greater extent, and production increases to a significantly smaller extent, than in most continental countries ...

The relatively low rate of increase of output and high rate of increase of prices may best be discussed in terms of labour supply, the growth of the capital stock and the course of profits and wages.

The relatively slow increase of output cannot be explained by differences in the growth of labour supply between the UK and other European countries. For while the average rate of growth of either the total labour force or employment ... has been substantially slower than in Germany, Italy and the Netherlands, it has been significantly higher than that prevailing in some of the faster growing countries such as Austria, France, Sweden and Norway ...

The share of 'productive' investment (defined here as non-residential construction, machinery and equipment) was considerably lower at the beginning of the period than in most industrialised European countries; it rose over the decade from 10 to 13 per cent of GNP, but it was still substantially lower at the end of the period than in the UK's main competitors ...

The relatively lower share of productive investment in the UK may have reflected a certain lack of confidence on the part of business. Private investment decisions are mainly determined by the views which business takes on final demand prospects and, more particularly on their competitive position *vis-à-vis* foreign producers. If costs and prices are seen to be rising faster at home than abroad, business confidence in the profitability of expanding capacity will begin to weaken ... In this sense, slow growth and modesty in investment decisions may progressively react on one another; an insufficiently keen competitive situation may tend to hold down investment and this, in turn, may tend to weaken the international competitive situation ...

But while productivity has risen more slowly in the UK than in most industrialised European countries, the same has not been true of money incomes. These, in fact, have risen appreciably faster than productivity, with a consequent increase in unit costs ...

The main increase in profits per unit of output has, generally, coincided with the periods of expanding output ... The increase in wages, on the other hand, while generally steepest when the labour market has been most strained, has remained high even when the demand for manpower has slackened ...

In short, pressure for higher money incomes has been permanent in the UK over the period and has resulted in increases which could not be absorbed without increases in unit costs. Restrictions upon demand, given the limits placed upon such a policy, have not provided a satisfactory solution.

*Economic Survey by the OECD: United Kingdom*, Paris, March 1962, pp. 10–20.

## 1.3 **Optimism in the 1960s**

> There was a general air of optimism in the first half of the 1960s that British growth performance could be improved by experiments in 'growth planning'. There is also a premonitory tone to this extract, especially on the balance of payments, which proved to be justified by events in 1964–66.

The first major report of the council[5] on the growth of the UK economy to 1966 ... was seen as establishing a framework which would itself be an important contribution to faster growth. It would help to make clear the way in which faster growth would impinge on the activities of many different branches of the economy ...

The 4 per cent objective involved setting sights for industrial output in almost all cases substantially above previous expectations. It also involved establishing objectives for public effort substantially above the level of government planning at the time ...

Demand has recently been growing at a rate of some 6 per cent per annum. During 1964 it is probable that demand will continue to increase at a high rate. There is likely to be a large increase in fixed investment, both public and private, a high level of stock building and a substantial growth of public consumption and consumer expenditure; exports should be helped by a continuing expansion of world trade although they are likely to grow more slowly than imports. In the circumstances there is likely to be a substantial increase in output and employment, and there are grounds for believing that there will be a good rise in productivity which could bring it close to the trend line implicit in the growth programme.

Output cannot, however, continue to increase indefinitely at the present high rate since this depends to a considerable extent on the bringing into use of underemployed resources and is more than the average rate required to achieve the growth programme during the rest of the period to 1966. Measures to adjust demand take time to have effect and any measures required to adjust demand to a sustainable rate of increase should be taken in good time so that they do not have to be too abrupt. There have been occasions in the past when a rapid economic recovery has been followed by years of more or less static production and productivity. The prospects are in certain respects more favourable on this occasion but achievement of sustainable economic expansion will involve the solution to difficult problems ...

For the growth programme to succeed the essential elements are a faster rise in productivity and in efficiency generally, a stable level of costs and prices, a more rapid growth in exports, and a lower growth of imports through more effective competition from home producers and economies in stockholding. There needs to be more training of skilled workers and a greater use made of the opportunities of expanding in the less prosperous regions which now contain much of the nation's remaining reserves of manpower. The modernisation of industry must be speeded up and more savings will be required to finance the growing investment of all kinds.

In the longer run the rate of growth that can be achieved will depend upon the extent to which new conditions can be created to secure a large and sustained rise in productivity. The next twelve to eighteen months will, however, present a particular challenge. There are fears that the cycle of rapid expansion followed by years of stagnation which has prevented sustained growth in the past will be repeated. There are opportunities this time of avoiding the difficulties which have checked growth in the past, but ... this will not be easy. It will require constructive effort in many directions and the widespread acceptance of new responsibilities. If it proves possible to break through the stop-go cycle[6] the confidence engendered, and its effect on investment and on willingness to accept measures to raise efficiency, should substantially improve the prospects for longer-term growth.

National Economic Development Council, *The Growth of the Economy*, London, 1964, pp. 1–8 (paras. 1, 6, 19–20, 43–4).

## 1.4 Deindustrialisation

In the early 1970s British commentators became dimly aware of a threat to faster growth from structural changes in the economy – the relative decline of manufacturing and the continuing rise in the proportion of total output contributed by the service sector. It became clear that other countries were experiencing similar trends but to a lesser extent than the UK.

Over the past fifteen years, manufacturing has become relatively less and less important in the total of economic activity ... [I]n 1965 manufacturing represented 34 per cent of the value of total output ... But by the early 1970s, the share had decline to around 30 per cent and by [1980] it was probably less than 25 per cent of the whole economy.

The decline has been sharply accentuated by the recession: in the year to the fourth quarter of 1980, manufacturing production dropped by about 15 per cent, the largest drop in any twelve-month period since the war. Over the same year, the work force in manufacturing dropped by 10 per cent compared with the average the previous year.

It is the decline in jobs which most worries people. Up to 1966, the absolute numbers employed in manufacturing were still rising. That year they hit a peak for the United Kingdom of 8.6 million. Ten years later, more than 1.3 million people had left manufacturing industry. Over the same period, the numbers employed in private services fluctuated but did not grow. The numbers employed in the public services rose steadily, although not by as much as the fall in jobs in manufacturing and other production industries ...

Now this curious transformation of the economy is not unique to Britain. Taking the years between 1960 and 1975, one finds that the

United States, Sweden, Holland and Belgium have all seen steady declines in the proportion of total employment in manufacturing. By contrast the proportion in Japan, Germany and Italy has risen – although in all three the rate of growth faltered by the middle 1970s ...

One of the first explanations of deindustrialisation to gain popularity was put forward by Robert Bacon and Walter Eltis[7] ... They laid the blame for the contraction of manufacturing on excessive government spending. At one level, their hypothesis was simply that the creation of jobs in the public sector had diverted manpower from the private sector. But this argument quickly evolved into a more sophisticated contention that the increasing claims of government had reduced the proportion available for consumption by the rest of the community.

The simplest version of the Bacon and Eltis thesis has never looked very convincing. It is hard to argue that successive public sector expansions have crippled industry by absorbing labour which manufacturing might otherwise have employed: ... it is men's jobs which have mainly been lost in manufacturing, while the 1970s expansion of the public sector largely created women's jobs.

Nor is it easy to believe that the private sector was held back by a shortage of funds – simply 'crowded out' of the capital market ...

But if deindustrialisation is not the fault of the growth of government, then what other explanation can there be? One possibility is that what we have seen is simply the old, familiar post-war problem of poor British competitiveness, manifested in a new form ... In 1955 the UK accounted for 20 per cent of world trade in manufactures. By 1976 that had declined to less than 9 per cent. Between 1960 and 1975, the UK share of world manufacturing output at constant prices fell from nearly 10 per cent to less than 6 per cent.

In the 1960s, everyone worried about Britain's falling share of the world market. In the 1970s, everyone began to worry about Britain's falling share of its own home market. Imported manufactured goods took about 8 per cent of the home market in 1961 and 13 per cent 10 years later. But while Britain's loss of world market share slowed down in the 1970s, import penetration accelerated. By 1976, imports were accounting for 21 per cent of the home market for manufactured goods.

If British industry had been more successful at fending off foreign competition, then it would have been able to increase output faster, and employment in manufacturing would probably have fallen much less rapidly than it has. But why has British industry found it so hard to compete? There are two answers, one old and one new.

Until the late 1970s, there was quite a lot of evidence that the problem was *not* that British manufacturers were too expensive, compared with foreign competition. Over the long run, exchange rate changes – the devaluation of the pound and the appreciation of the currencies of our strongest competitors – roughly balanced the tendency of British costs to rise faster than those of other countries. So it looks as though Britain's failure to compete successfully in the world market and at home is the result of something other than price.

The UK car industry epitomises the problem. It is one of the industries where world market share has been lost most dramatically, where imports have grown fastest, and where the decline in labour has been most striking. Yet British cars have not, over most of the past fifteen years, been wildly overpriced compared with foreign competitors. They seem to have suffered from a reputation for poor reliability, inability to keep delivery dates, bad distribution of spare parts, and unimaginative design.

These problems are not simply the result of low investment, or bad labour relations, or restrictive practices and overmanning, or the low status of middle management and the poor pay of production engineers in Britain. But all these things put together have produced an industry incapable of holding its own against the better-organised industries of Japan, or West Germany, or the United States.

That is the old problem of competitiveness. But, of course, the late 1970s saw the emergence of a new one. By the end of 1980, it was no longer true that the exchange rate compensated firms for loss of competitiveness. From a peak in 1977, UK competitiveness[8] fell by 65 per cent by the end of 1980. The appreciation of the pound coincided with a rapid rise in labour costs, faster than that in most other industrial countries.

There are two possible explanations for this massive loss of competitiveness. One blames it on interest rates. The other blames it on North Sea oil ...

There are only two ways to halt the appreciation [of sterling which has caused the loss of competitiveness]. One is to encourage an outflow of capital – to invest the proceeds of North Sea oil abroad. That would put the burden of adjustment on the capital account of the balance of payments[9] and would mean that, when the oil runs out, we might be able to live on the earnings from our investments abroad. The only alternative is to expand the economy – to try to create demand at home which will offset the loss of demand for our manufactures overseas.

Each course has its drawbacks. There is a widely held view that more investment abroad means less capital for British industry. This is nonsense: what holds back investment in Britain is the poor rate which investors can earn on their money, and that in turn is a reflection of the poor profitability of British industry. But investing abroad means taking a risk that the investment will be safe and that its profits will eventually come back to Britain.

Expanding the economy to boost demand faces a different set of risks: the danger that inflation might once again take off, for instance, and the danger that no expansion could be large enough to offset the impact on the balance of payments of another big jump in the price of oil. But the problem of the strong pound, whatever its causes, has merely aggravated the decline in manufacturing employment ...

To sum up, deindustrialisation appears to be a new name for the old British problem of uncompetitive manufacturing. It is a problem which has been exacerbated by the appreciation of sterling. Its causes lie in the structure of British industry, in the quality of management and the tradition of labour relations. There are no easy cures ... If manufacturing industry became more competitive, then it might still shed jobs: but at least it would be easier for the rest of the economy to replace them.

Frances Cairncross, 'Where have all the jobs gone?', *The Guardian*, Monday 6 April 1981.

## 1.5 The Thatcher 'economic miracle' of the 1980s

After a deep recession from 1979 to 1981 the economy began to recover and experienced a long, sustained upswing. The architect of Thatcherite economic policy was Nigel Lawson, Chancellor of the Exchequer from 1983 to 1989. This is part of his assessment of the Thatcherite economic record.

Looking back on my decade of office from 1979 to 1989, two main themes emerge, one political and one economic ...

The economic theme is that free-market Toryism proved both a success in the UK and a beacon to much of the rest of the world; and that my own stewardship, whatever its shortcomings, was an important part of that success ... I still believe that we were in many ways pioneering, and most certainly reinforcing, a trend which has swept the world, including the former communist countries, and which had not run its course by the early 1990s ...

The most popular yardstick of economic performance over a run of years is ... real economic growth. The official statistics of the UK's growth performance over the quarter century to 1989 are summarised in the table ... which is shown in terms of complete economic cycles, so that an entirely fair comparison can be made, undistorted by cyclical factors. I have also added a breakdown of the pre-1989 cycle into two periods[10] broadly corresponding to the tenure as Chancellor of Geoffrey Howe and myself ...

**UK economic growth** (average annual growth rates, per cent)

| | *1964–73* | *1973–79* | *1979–89* | *1979–83* | *1983–89* |
|---|---|---|---|---|---|
| Real GDP | 3 | 1½ | 2¼ | ¼ | 3½ |
| Non-oil real GDP | 3 | ¾ | 2¼ | –¼ | 3¾ |
| Output per head | | | | | |
| Manufacturing | 3¾ | ¾ | 4¼ | 3½ | 4¾ |
| Whole economy | 3 | 1¼ | 1¾ | 2 | 1¾ |
| Non-North Sea economy | 3 | ¾ | 1¾ | 1¾ | 2 |

Interpretation of the table is considerably affected by the treatment of North Sea oil and gas output. While its contribution to GDP is frequently exaggerated – even at its peak it accounted for little more than 5 per cent – its dramatic rise from virtually nothing, and its subsequent decline, make a considerable difference to the growth statistics. Oil was a big plus factor for Labour in 1973–79, and at best neutral for the Conservatives in 1979–89. The output of the North Sea is not to be sneezed at, but it is to a large extent a windfall, yielding a surplus well above production costs ... Excluding oil, growth was considerably faster in the Howe-Lawson cycle of 1979–89 than in the largely Labour cycle of 1973–9 which preceded it.

Any assessment of the growth record also needs to take account of the world slow-down which followed the first oil price explosion of 1973. The international data ... shows that growth rates slowed down everywhere – not merely in 1973–79, but in 1979–89 as well. Against this background Britain's growth performance in the 1980s emerges quite creditably.

Looking at the productivity figures in the table, defined in terms of output per head, performance during the 1980s was also significantly better than it was in the previous cycle. Ironically, it was entirely due to the sparkling performance of manufacturing industry, whose productivity improved even faster than in the pre-1973 oil shock cycle – particularly during my own period as Chancellor. This was the sector of the economy of which the Conservatives in general, and I in particular, were regularly accused of at best neglecting, if not of subjecting to an actively anti-manufacturing policy. Once again, UK performance in the 1980s looks even better in the context of the overall world picture, since our competitors achieved no similar spectacular improvement.

Nor was the sharp improvement in manufacturing productivity achieved at the expense of a declining manufacturing base, as the Labour Party frequently alleged.[11] Indeed, the boot was on the other foot. It is indeed true that, for some time, manufacturing in Britain has been declining as a proportion of total output – and even more as a proportion of employment – as indeed it has in almost all advanced industrialised countries. But in absolute terms, whereas manufacturing output fell by 5 per cent over the overwhelmingly Labour 1973–79 cycle, it rose by 12 per cent over the Conservative 1979–89 cycle – the entire rise occurring, again ironically, during my time as Chancellor ...

The big puzzle, at first sight, is why, by contrast, the recorded figures for productivity growth outside manufacturing, notably in the service sector, were so unimpressive during the 1979–89 cycle. There is, in fact, a simple explanation. The 1980s were characterised by a massive growth in part-time employment, almost exclusively in the fast-growing service sector, and largely composed of married women. Clearly a part-time worker cannot be expected to produce as much as a full-time worker. Thus the productivity record outside manufacturing, and hence also for the economy as a whole, would look considerably better in the 1980s were it not for the CSO's eccentric failure to distinguish between full-time and part-time workers. This also, incidentally, affects the international comparisons, since there was no comparable explosion of part-time employment among our major overseas competitors. In other words, the UK's record in the 1980s looked at in the world context would emerge even better were the CSO to calculate productivity on a less bizarre basis ...

In addition to neglecting manufacturing, the government was widely accused of neglecting industrial investment. It is true that in my first budget I reformed company taxation and removed the tax bias in favour of investment in industrial plant and equipment. But on the reasonable proposition that the proof of the pudding is in the eating, the latter charge of neglect is as much a myth as the former ... [as] there was a dramatic acceleration in fixed investment in the 1980s, compared with the lamentable performance over the 1973–79 cycle – indeed, investment grew significantly faster than consumption during the Conservative cycle.

This acceleration was particularly marked in non-housing investment. Business investment, which had risen by around 3 per cent a year over both the 1964–73 and 1973–79 cycles, increased by 5 per cent a year over the 1979–89 cycle. During my own period as Chancellor – that is, for the most part, after my allegedly anti-investment corporation tax reform – it rose by 8.5 per cent a year. A further irony, incidentally, is that the miserable overall investment performance during the predominantly Labour cycle of 1973–79 was largely due to a sharp decline in public sector non-housing investment – that is, schools, hospitals and the infrastructure – which was reversed by the Thatcher government.

Nigel Lawson, *The View from No. 11: Memoirs of a Tory Radical*, London, 1993, pp. 975–9.

## 1.6 The slump of 1990–92

This second extract from an OECD survey of the UK economy shows that the upswing of the 1980s became increasingly feverish and produced a significant contraction of output as economic agents began to readjust to world market conditions.

*The origins of excess demand*

The UK economy entered a period of severe overheating in early 1987. Over the two-year period 1987–88, the growth of total domestic demand averaged some 7 to 8 per cent a year and that of real GDP almost 4.5 ... By early 1988, the level of aggregate demand had probably surpassed that of potential output. This excessive rate of demand expansion reflected *inter alia* booming investment and buoyant household demand, underpinned by strong growth in borrowing, particularly mortgage credit. The aggregate rate of unemployment subsequently dropped below 6 per cent in 1989 and cost and price pressures intensified.

Macroeconomic policies failed to check the overheating of the economy. The conduct of macroeconomic policy was marred by poor macroeconomic data and persistent forecasting errors. An optimistic assessment of what had been achieved through structural reform in raising *underlying* productivity growth also led to strong private sector confidence. The rapid emergence of excess demand took many analysts by surprise.

One factor in the unexpectedly strong expansion of demand was the interplay of financial market liberalisation, asset price inflation and the emergence of excessive private sector debt levels.[12] The rise in UK house prices relative to prices generally was the most pronounced among G–5 countries,[13] leading to a marked rise in household wealth levels ... This no doubt influenced the sharp drop in the personal sector's savings rate,[14] from a peak of over 13 per cent in 1980, to less than 5 per cent by 1988. From 1981 to 1988, personal debt grew extremely rapidly: mortgage debt rose from 30 to 70 per cent of disposable income, by far the highest ratio among G–5 countries. A significant part of this borrowing may have been channelled to finance consumption rather than housing: 'equity withdrawal' from loans originally made for house purchases is estimated to have been nearly £25 billion in 1988 alone (roughly 5 per cent of GDP). The housing boom triggered a surge in consumption despite high interest rates, and an unprecedented household deficit emerged in 1988 ...

Business investment rose by 43 per cent in the three years to 1989, bolstered by rising real rates of return, rapid growth of output, buoyant business confidence and high rates of capacity utilisation. The investment boom was largely debt financed. It was sustained by enhanced access to financing facilities ... All in all, given the build-up of excessive household and corporate sector debt levels, a correction in spending and asset prices became inevitable, although its size and timing were difficult to predict.

*The current recession*

Domestic demand proved surprisingly resilient until mid–1990, despite base lending rates progressively rising from 7.5 per cent in May 1988 to 15 per cent by October 1989 and remaining at that level until October 1990 ... Domestic demand fell in the second half of 1990, ... start[ing] with a cut-back of interest-sensitive components of expenditure. New car sales plummeted by some 16 per cent from their year earlier levels in the last quarter of 1990, compounded by higher petrol prices and uncertainty related to the Gulf conflict. Residential housing and related consumer durables were also depressed by sharply increasing debt service[15] and deteriorating household balance-sheet positions.[16] A drop in house prices and an easing in financial market prices quickly turned the cut-back in spending into recession, with building societies reporting sharp increases in mortgage defaults ...

The drop in private consumption and high interest rates worsened already heavily geared[17] corporate balance sheets, and the Gulf conflict increased private sector uncertainty. With corporate profits under sharp pressure, and rising bankruptcies, business investment was scaled back in the second half of 1990. Investment in the manufacturing and non-residential construction sectors, where over-capacity and over-building had emerged, has been cut back significantly ...

The fall in total domestic demand, when it eventually came in mid–1990, was far sharper than expected by almost all observers ...

Unlike the 1980–81 recession, which was concentrated in the tradeable good sector,[18] the current recession has been more widespread between regions and sectors, albeit still hitting manufacturing industries hard. By the last quarter of 1990, output of all production industries had dropped by almost 4.5 per cent from its second quarter peak, and 3.5 per cent from its year earlier level. The drop in manufacturing has been of a similar magnitude, with output continuing to fall into the first quarter of 1991 albeit at a somewhat slower rate. The decline in the construction sector came later, but was even more pronounced through the course of 1990. In contrast to the 1980–81 recession, the drop in the distributive trades, hotels and catering, and transport and communications was almost as pronounced in the second half of 1990 as that of the goods-producing industries.

*OECD Economic Surveys, 1990–91: United Kingdom*, Paris, 1991, pp. 11–18.

# 2
# Industrial performance

Having looked at aggregate economic performance, our attention shifts to individual industries and sectors. This is not a happy story. Britain's relative economic decline has been based upon competitive weakness in key branches of the economy, notably in the heavier, 'metal-bashing' parts of manufacturing and the 'old staples' of coal and cotton. There have also been brighter spots within manufacturing and, especially, services, as the following extracts illustrate.

## 2.1 Conditions in the British coal industry in 1944

The coal industry was a persistent problem during wartime. In September 1944 a committee of specialist mining engineers was set up to assess the industry's prospects.

Our comparison of conditions in the coal industries of certain other countries with those in Britain leads us to draw the following conclusions:

(1) Natural conditions in Britain are greatly inferior to those found in the USA. They are, however, comparable with those of the Ruhr and Holland, and, therefore, afford no explanation of the much lower OMS[1] obtained in Britain.

(2) Continental industries have been able to command adequate financial resources with which to carry out major technical improvements and have also been helped by more favourable taxation arrangements than in Britain. The British industry, as a whole, has been in a perpetual state of financial embarrassment, and the long-standing uncertainty surrounding the future ownership of the industry[2] has not been conducive to expenditure on long-term

improvements necessary to raise the general efficiency of the industry.

(3) In Britain, the fact that ownership of the mineral has been in private hands has often resulted in unduly small or awkwardly shaped leaseholds;[3] in the development of an excessive number of mines of insufficient capacity for the requirements of the best mining practice; and in inadequate attention to the conservation of the national resources ... On the continent, the mineral has been owned by the state, and both concessions and individual mines have generally been large.

(4) The grouping of a number of mines under the same ownership on the continent has facilitated the closing down, or merging, of uneconomic mines, and the concentration of operations to the remaining shafts. In Britain, ownership is widely dispersed, and this avenue to greater efficiency has never been explored on any adequate scale.

(5) The layout of the continental mines with straight level roads[4] driven through the strata provided a foundation for reorganisation of the underground workings. In Britain the undulating and often circuitous roadways extending far from the shafts require more drastic and more difficult reconstruction for the attainment of full efficiency.

(6) The fact that pneumatic picks are widely used in the Ruhr and Holland, while coalcutters are used in Britain, does not provide an explanation of the higher OMS obtained in these coalfields ...

(7) The use of locomotive haulage on straight level roads driven through the strata on the continent (and in solid coal in the USA), instead of the traditional haulage systems used in Britain, constitutes one of the greatest single technical causes of the lower OMS in British mines compared with that of the Ruhr or Holland.

(8) There has been no properly organised training of entrants into the British coal-mining industry. In contrast, a thorough training is provided in Holland and Germany.

(9) In Britain, in contrast to the continent, sizes of coal are not standardised nor qualities adequately classified. An excessive multiplication of qualities and sizes, especially in relation to house coals, has had unfortunate effects upon the efficiency of mining and surface operations.

(10) The employers, as a body, have been prepared neither to accept the principle of the survival of the fittest nor fully abandon

their traditional individualism. In relation to their own undertakings, the short view has all too often prevailed.

(11) The British mining engineers have often been handicapped by this short-term view and have not usually enjoyed the technical independence evidently allowed to mining engineers on the continent. Far too few of them, however, appreciated the extent of reorganisation required, either because of an unduly conservative outlook, or because of a lack of awareness of what needed to be done.

(12) In Britain there has, with certain exceptions, been a lack of co-operation between the mineworkers and employers. In particular the British mineworker has not usually accepted the machine as a necessity. With fuller co-operation OMS would have been considerably higher than it was.

Ministry of Fuel and Power, *Coal Mining: Report of the Technical Advisory Committee* (the Reid report), London, 1945 (Cmd 6610), pp. 37–8.

## 2.2 Agriculture immediately after the war

Agriculture received a positive stimulus from war in the form of increased government subsidies for production. In the difficult post-war balance of payments position and in the face of a world food shortage, still higher levels of agricultural output were needed.

The net output of British agriculture increased by about 35 per cent during the war; intensive mechanisation made British agriculture one of the most highly mechanised in the world, with 190,000 tractors compared with the pre-war 60,000; output per man-year rose by 10–15 per cent. The problem now is to adjust the industry to post-war needs, while retaining the wartime gains in efficiency and developing them still further.

The government's policy, both to save foreign exchange and for good farming, is to switch our production, as rapidly as the cereals position permits, from the production of crops for direct human consumption to the production of livestock and livestock products, especially pigs and poultry. The import of £1,000 worth of feeding stuffs will save nearly £2,000 worth of imports of livestock products.

The world cereal shortage[5] has delayed this policy. This year we must still have a large production of wheat, potatoes and sugar-beet, and the target acreages are similar to those of 1945. Except for milk, the supply of which is steadily increasing, output of livestock products in the year from 1 June 1947 will be little above that of the current livestock year ...

More agricultural workers are required. We shall soon be losing the 130,000 prisoners of war, one-half of whom are in effect regular workers. The government's plan for getting foreign labour ... should help.[6] But the long-term solution can lie only in the establishment of a prosperous and highly efficient agriculture. The government will take what steps it can to provide more houses for agricultural workers. The agricultural machinery industry is expanding, and foreign exchange is allowed for the import of machines required for improving efficiency; the further increase of output per man-year offers the best prospect of satisfying the industry's manpower problems.

*Economic Survey for 1947*, London, 1947 (Cmd 7046), p. 24.

## 2.3 Comparative inefficiency in the British cotton textile industry

In 1948 the Labour government helped to establish the Anglo-American Council on Productivity, which sponsored visits by teams from British industry to their counterparts in the USA. These are the principal conclusions of the cotton textiles team.

In our opinion, the high productivity of mills in the USA is largely due to the following causes:

(1) Productivity mindedness of management, supervisory staff and operatives resulting from the realisation that the high standard of living apparent on every hand in America and the eventual security of employment depend on producing more at home at a lower cost rather than less at a higher cost. Textile unions support a policy of high productivity for the same reasons.

(2) Willingness on the part of managements and operatives to give a fair trial to new machines and new methods rather than to rely on experiments made by others ...

(3) Widespread use of standards against which the realised performances of men, machines and raw material can be measured at every stage of manufacture, thus ensuring the prompt detection of faults and the pinpointing of their source. Intelligent use of standards counterbalances the lessened machine supervision by operatives which is entailed in the spreading of labour over a larger number of machines.

(4) Recognition by managements of the valuable services which reliable firms of consulting engineers can render ...

(5) Exchange of technical information between rival firms engaged in the same business.

(6) Good relations between managements and labour, resulting from a positive policy and effort on the part of managements, which emanates from the top and is carried right through the mill ...

(7) The acceptance by operatives and unions of the principle that work assignments should be based on a fair work load and not an arbitrary number of machines or spindles tended. To obtain the correct work assignment and to narrow the field of possible dispute, trained work study men are required. They are employed by both management and by unions in the USA.[7]

(8) Recognition in the USA that the work assignment in terms of machines or spindles tended, or duties to be performed, should be changed as, and when, justified by the introduction of new machinery ...

(9) Staff promotion by merit. High technical qualifications are preferred while practical experience, not only as an apprentice or as an overseer, but also for a time, at least, as a working operative, is regarded as essential. Promotion for operatives is by seniority but with automatic relegation for those who fail to make the grade after a reasonable trial period.

(10) The attachment of proper importance to employment and personnel departments which deal with recommendations for hiring and dismissal, induction, personal records, job training, technical education, absenteeism and labour turnover.

(11) Good provision for technological training for all grades and thorough on-the-job training for new operatives who are taught the best methods by instructors who have themselves been well trained as teachers ...

(15) The use of good costing systems which have mostly been introduced in the past thirty years and are on more standardised

lines than in England. A costing system with budgetary control not only provides information as to which lines are the most profitable, but also gives accurate and up-to-date information as to how productivity can be increased and costs lowered.

(16) Simplification by limitation of the yarn counts spun ...

(17) Three-shift working making it easier to justify expenditure on new machinery and labour-saving devices. It also emphasises the need for the improved utilisation of labour. The cost of labour is greater in the USA than in England, both absolutely and relatively to the cost of machinery ...

(18) The allocation of considerable sums from profits ... for the purchase of machinery. This is necessary as, despite three-shift working, depreciation is allowed at a rate ranging from 3 per cent to 6 per cent per annum. American managements are intensely cost-conscious when purchasing machinery. Old machinery, modernised as and when desirable, remains in use until the purchase of new machinery can be shown to be an economic proposition.

(19) The use of the pick of American raw cotton ensuring great regularity of grade, staple, character and continuity of supply ... At the present date, spinners in England have to pay a higher premium than spinners in the USA for the types which are desired by mills using short processing and sometimes these types are not obtainable at all ...[8]

(20) The use, wherever possible, of mechanical aids and labour-saving devices, such as travelling overhead ceiling blowers in card rooms, overhead cleaners in ring rooms, pneumatic roller pickers in card and ring rooms and many others ...

(21) Good machine maintenance.

*Productivity Team Report on Cotton Spinning* (Anglo-American Council on Productivity), London, 1950, pp. 5–6.

## 2.4 A progressive steel firm in the 1950s

By no means all British firms have suffered continuously from blinkered management and obstructive unions. The Department of Scientific and Industrial Research published a series of pamphlets in the 1950s to illustrate good practice. This extract is taken from the first, describing the recent history of a long-established steel firm.

Beyond doubt this company has introduced technical changes in the last thirty years without causing any of the big conflicts that sometimes arise. The trade unions have accepted each innovation and expansion, and the men have acquiesced in and adapted themselves to the change, even if they have not always approved of it. The unions have never refused to help the company adjust a partly redundant labour force, though they did refuse to help select men for transfer to the new melting shop.

This does not mean that the men, or their representatives, liked all the results of change. Several cases of dissatisfaction have been noted ... yet, except for the case of the post-war craftsmen, they did not lead to open conflict, either when technical change was first proposed or during the long period of adaptation. And the general attitude, seen in retrospect, was one of widespread approval. A majority of 'survivors' of each change claimed that it made them better off on the whole, and a fair number of even the lowest occupational groups were prepared to approve a hypothetical case of innovation, although it caused redundancy. Of course, no one should rely too much on the predictive value of these statements.

Adaptation has been fairly easy in this company because the social consequences of technical change were not so radical as to affect adversely any big group of production workers. Although minorities have suffered, especially among older employees, there have been no sweeping changes for the majority. In general, earnings have remained high, the seniority principle has been retained, and there has been little change in the relative distribution of rewards between grades. Similarly, teamwork, and a big output bonus based on it, remain principles of work organisation.

The harmony of management-union relations has also helped to reduce possible conflict. Each side recognises certain functions as legitimate and appropriate to it. Thus the trade unions have conceded the right of management to make technical changes and, if it so wishes, to select labour for new processes. Likewise the company has recognised the unions' claim to determine seniority and to help in arrangements for promotion.

A number of problems arising from technical change have been handled within the unions and so have not occasioned conflict between them and the management. It is probable that the machinery for handling grievances has helped to ease the process of change, since it has developed over so many years and now works smoothly. Within a broad system of national agreements the union officials on the shop floor have wide powers and can deal very quickly with disagreements or grievances.

Economic factors have also helped. The steel industry has a very high ratio of capital costs to labour costs, and a modern steel plant must be kept running continuously both for this reason and because coke ovens, blast furnaces and open hearth furnaces can suffer big losses and considerable damage if they are allowed to cool before adequate precautions have been taken. These two factors – relatively low labour costs and the need for continuous running – have also helped to keep wages high; and high wages, along with the seniority principle, give employees a big stake in the company and strongly disincline them to hinder its operations ...

Craftsmen are in a different position. Increased in numbers and importance, they tend to believe that their rewards are no longer adequate. In the past they have given allegiance to their crafts rather than to the industry or the company, and only in recent years have they begun to appreciate, in their relations with management, the special position and problems of craftsmen in steel. What is more, they depend less on the company than production workers, because seniority matters less to them and because they are more mobile both inside and outside the company. Their mobility makes them more militant than production workers and helps to determine their whole attitude to technical change.

Smooth adaptation to change has depended on the company's policies as well as high earnings, the seniority system and other characteristic features of the industry. For example, although the company could have manned the new processes from any source, it gave preference to existing employees and so caused little or no redundancy. It paid attention to the existing pattern of seniority when determining the rank of each man transferred to a new job. The management was always ready to discuss problems with representatives of employees, and these discussions continually helped it to decide on both the principles and the details of action. To employees who could not be reabsorbed in the new melting shop it offered jobs in the coke ovens and the blast furnace on conditions that were generous compared with those of similar units elsewhere. Finally, it planned the technical changes well in advance and introduced them in phases. This greatly simplified the handling of transitional problems.

Department of Scientific and Industrial Research, *Men, Steel and Technical Change* (Problems of Progress in Industry, 1), London, 1957, pp. 33–5.

## 2.5 Machine tools in the mid–1960s

> Signs of competitive weakness were becoming painfully obvious in the mid–1960s in this key industry, which was an important 'carrier' of technological change throughout manufacturing. The production and export targets in this 'action programme' for the period 1964–70 were particularly ambitious.

*Output, manpower and output per head*

Output is expected to rise by 57 per cent between 1964 and 1970, compared with an increase of just over 8 per cent in the period 1960–64. This represents a forecast annual growth rate of 7.8 per cent as against 2.0 per cent for the 1960–64 period ...

It is expected that manpower requirements will rise by nearly 19 per cent or 12,000 by 1970, compared with a growth of less than 7 per cent between 1960–64 ... The industry is confident that it can recruit this labour force by 1970, though it expects that supply may be difficult in the interim ...

Increases are expected in qualified scientists and technologists, whose numbers are expected to double from 950 to 1,800, and in supporting technical staff, from 5,100 to 8,200 or from 8 per cent to 11 per cent of the total labour force. At the same time, the requirement for skilled craftsmen and comparable workers ... is expected to lessen slightly: this would apply especially to fitters, erectors and turners, though there will be simultaneously an increasing demand for semi-skilled assemblers and machine operators.

New investment is expected to increase sharply up to 1967 and to be maintained at a high level ...

*Exports and imports*

Production for export rose at 7.0 per cent annually at constant prices from 1960 to 1964 with the share of total production rising from 25 per cent to 31 per cent. The forecast production for export in 1970 is £69 million, an annual rise of 10.5 per cent from 1964 to 1970 and a 36 per cent share of production in 1970.

Imports have been rising somewhat faster than exports. Imports rose by approximately 11 per cent per annum at constant prices from 1960 to 1964, and their share of total supply grew from 21 per cent to 28 per cent. The industry's action programme[9] should help to improve the balance of trade.

*Technological changes*

The major technological change in the industry and its customer industries is the spread of electronically controlled tools. The co-operation of the machine tool industry with the electronics industry and with other supplier industries is likely to grow closer in the future; the influx of fresh thinking which this could bring, together with the increasing concentration on design, should prove particularly stimulating to the machine tool industry, as to all production engineering functions. The spread of numerical control will also reduce the number of skilled setter-operators, etc., and allow semi-skilled operators to tend more than one machine. Intensive working of these expensive tools is necessary to make them economic, and this underlines the importance of the trade union commitment under the action programme to support the maximum use of high-productivity equipment ...

*Structural changes*

At present the UK machine tool industry consists of about 200 firms, the main geographical concentrations being in London, Birmingham-Coventry, south Lancashire and the Halifax area of Yorkshire. A substantial number of the total are already members of larger groupings, with interests either in general engineering or solely in machine tools, and have the backing of these groups financially, in design and in their export efforts. Many are, however, small but size alone is no criterion of efficiency. So long as its research and design are concentrated on a relatively narrow field, a small firm may make a useful contribution. However, some small companies are too weak to mount the necessary effort and so do not use the scarce skilled labour to the best effect. Some rationalisation appears called for.

*The National Plan*, London, 1965 (Cmnd 2764), part 2, pp. 95–7.

## 2.6 Problems in the shipbuilding industry

British shipbuilders conspicuously failed to exploit favourable market conditions in the 1950s and 1960s. A government-inspired rationalisation of the mid-1960s failed in the early 1970s, and a new survey of the industry was commissioned from outside industrial consultants. This is an extract from their report.

**4 Many of the industry's long-term difficulties will only be resolved by strengthening the present weaknesses in general management.**

*(1) There is a shortage of managerial ability in the industry, particularly in non-technical areas*
Most managers have technical backgrounds and lack skills in commercial areas. The main emphasis is placed on design and production with a corresponding neglect of functions such as marketing, finance and control. Few companies market actively; in the financial area, management accounting in particular is inadequate.

Shortage of managerial ability is also reflected in the low priority given to support functions such as personnel, labour relations and management services. This is particularly significant since poor delivery performance is often blamed on bad industrial relations. In addition the ability to deliver on time must be closely related to effective planning and control.

The lack of general management skills is in part due to the industry's insular attitudes and neglect of internal management development. Few managers have been recruited from other industries with experience of similar management problems, such as civil engineering; further, the industry has been static and has not appeared to offer attractive career opportunities.

While craft training has been well supported, management development has not. In general, opportunities to educate potential managers in non-technical skills have not been taken.

There are, of course, notable exceptions to these comments. Selected companies are developing strong management teams and major improvements are being made.

*(2) In most spheres of activity the industry lacks information in a form which provides a sound basis for management decisions*
The industry has insufficient information on the market in which it is operating. Too little is known of foreign competition: systematic market research effort is limited; potential sources of information such as brokers are not always fully uitilised. As a result, the main source of shipbuilders' information about the market is shipowner inquiries.

The industry is also hampered by the lack of an adequate measure of output. The conventional measures, gross, deadweight and steel tonnage have severe limitations ...

Allied with the problem of measuring output is the problem of measuring productivity. Man-hours per ton of steel appear to be a relevant measure of steel work efficiency for a given type and size of ship. It cannot, however, be used for industry-wide comparisons. Nor is it relevant to non-steel work activities in which many of the production problems occur.

Most companies generate sufficient information internally, but rarely process it into a form which presents a clear and concise picture of the company's position. Information tends to be in such detail that a comprehensive overview is difficult to attain. Poor internal information systems also result in an inadequate data base for such functions as estimating, planning and budgeting.

*(3) The industry fails to plan adequately at both the strategic and the detailed levels*
Top management rarely defines corporate objectives or formulates corporate strategies to direct the company's future development. Instead management tends to concentrate on short-term issues, and major decisions are made on an 'ad hoc' basis rather than within established policy guidelines.

Despite the long time cycle involved in building ships, few companies prepare comprehensive plans which cover all functions.

Manpower planning is virtually unknown, market planning is rarely done, and profit and loss projections are seldom prepared for more than one year in advance. The few companies which prepare long-term plans tend to concentrate on facilities with little regard for the financial and manpower implications or the market.

[C]ontract planning is weak and individual contract plans are rarely integrated into an overall company plan. Again planning is rarely comprehensive.

The planning function tends to suffer from low status in the organisation and from top management's negative attitudes. It too often suffers from a poor information base.

*(4) Management does not exercise close control over company activities*

The industry's shortcomings in managerial resources, information and planning have led to weakened control of company activities. This has been highlighted in recent years by the industry's poor delivery and profit performance.

In addition, few companies have prepared contingency plans to reduce the impact of factors outside their direct control, but which influence the company's performance, such as late delivery of materials, inflation and national strikes.

Department of Trade and Industry, *British Shipbuilding 1972: A Report to the Department of Trade and Industry by Booz Allen & Hamilton International BV*, London, 1973, pp. 6–7.

## 2.7 The British motor manufacturing industry

It became obvious in the mid–1970s that the British motor industry was in crisis, and British-owned firms were in the deepest mess. Several official investigations were undertaken. This is an extract from the report of the House of Commons Expenditure Committee.

*Manufacturing efficiency*

The chairman of Ford told us 'in this business we need economies of scale to remain profitable'. Mr Beckett went on to say that world competition meant that there were real problems for small-volume producers of cars. We were told privately by two witnesses that the development of an entirely new car might cost £50 million and the development of a new model using existing major components and some existing pressings could cost not less than half that figure.[10] So the incentive to spread research, design and tooling costs as widely as possible is clearly very strong. Ford's ability to combine their

British and German volumes to minimise the impact of costs has clearly benefited them ...

In addition to, and sometimes intensifying, the problem of achieving scale economies is the problem of under-utilisation of capacity. This ought to be a temporary phenomenon, but ... it has been an area in which British industry has been chronically inefficient. Ford identified this as 'the most single important factor' in their poor return on capital. This is a problem of a different type from that of poor scale economy. Low returns on capital resulting from too small an operation to generate sufficient economies of scale can be improved by an increase in size, which is a long-term process. Working below capacity can have a number of causes. Ford identified their particular problem as one of industrial relations. However, whether the cause is lack of demand, supply difficulties, or industrial relations, the resulting low return on capital is capable of correction in the short term if early attention is paid to the problem giving rise to it.

BLMC[11] has suffered from both the difficulties described in [the previous] paragraphs. Although the Corporation has the size to take advantage of considerable economies of scale, it has suffered from all three of the principal causes of the under-utilisation of capacity ...

'Overmanning', frequently identified as a cause of inefficiency, is a term which confuses two different things. The first is the comparatively high labour-intensity of the British motor industry. This has been very largely the result of the lack of investment. Workers are employed to do jobs which in other countries are generally performed by capital equipment, and manning levels are high as a result. The Ryder report[12] attributed the use in BLMC's car operations of considerably more manpower than the theoretical standard manpower required partly to the use of old and outdated plant and machinery ...

The second type of overmanning is quite simply the employment of more men than are needed to do the job with existing equipment, whatever the technically appropriate capital/labour ratio might be. The SMMT[13] felt that there was scope for an overall reduction in the numbers employed, and the evidence of a number of witnesses suggested that this type of overmanning exists in the industry. Mr Lowry[14] said that BLMC had an element of overmanning in a number of plants which was being tackled very vigorously. During the course of our inquiry Ford suffered a dispute at Dagenham which was at least partly a result of an attempt to reduce manning levels. The Ryder report gave 'currently agreed manning levels' as a second reason for the use by BLMC of more workers than was theoretically necessary. One manufacturer put manning in a major plant complex at 10 per cent above requirements ... the TGWU agreed that the industry employed more men than the absolute minimum to do the job, but Mr Evans[15] pointed out that this was because labour turnover and absenteeism through sickness had to be allowed for. He thought that in this context the industry did not employ surplus labour. Men may stand idle when a new model is being introduced or when technical problems arise but this does not mean that the company can dispense with them.

It is misleading to describe as 'overmanned' an operation which is labour-intensive, and, for the reasons pointed out by the TGWU, an effective labour force must employ more men than the theoretical minimum needed for the job. However, we suspect that in some cases these reasons may have proved a convenient excuse for those who have not achieved or who have resisted reductions in manning levels.

*Fourteenth Report from the Expenditure Committee: The Motor Vehicle Industry*, House of Commons Sessional Papers 1974–75, London, 1975, pp. 40–3.

## 2.8 Travel and tourism

As commentators began to perceive the relative decline in manufacturing, interest grew in the output, employment and balance of payments potential of the service sector.

About two-fifths of our total export earnings are now provided by 'invisible' credits[16] to which travel and tourism contribute an important share.

In 1974 Britain's tourist receipts came to an estimated £830 million, or £1,070 million when fare payments by overseas visitors to British air and sea carriers are included. This £1,070 million represented 10.7 per cent of our total invisible receipts and 4.1 per cent of our total exports, visible and invisible, compared with 10.1 per cent and 3.8 per cent respectively in 1968. Figures so far available for 1975 indicate a marked expansion over 1974. During recent years Britain's tourist industry has received heavy investment, with government assistance. Consequently, it has the capacity for considerable further expansion …

*Tourist earnings and payments*
Up to the late 1960s, Britain usually ran an annual deficit on its international tourist account. This was because our receipts from overseas visitors fell well below the spending by UK visitors to other countries. This pattern has radically altered and, in recent years, the expansion of our tourist earnings has outstripped tourist payments. In 1973, exceptionally, the balance (excluding fare payments) was even, due to a big increase in UK spending overseas. But in 1974 there was a large surplus of £150 million.[17]

*Number of visitors and area pattern*
Over the past eight years the number of visits to Britain has climbed from 4.3 million in 1967 to 7.9 million in 1974. Between 1973 and 1974 the overall increase of 3 per cent was smaller than usual. This was mainly because the number of visitors from North America fell by 15 per cent and accounted for only 22 per cent of the total inflow as against 27 per cent in 1973. On the other hand, the number of visitors from EEC countries went up by 7 per cent and accounted for almost half of all visitors in 1974 …

*Changes in recent years*
Between 1967 and 1974 the average length of stay of overseas visitors in Britain has fallen fairly steadily from 17.1 days to 13.9 days. Over the same period the average expenditure per day has gone up from £3.10p to £7.50p, and average expenditure per visit from £52.50p to £105.10p.

In 1973 (the latest year for which detailed country figures are available) average expenditure per visit was £64.50p for western European visitors as a whole and £99.20p for North America. Visitors from South Africa and from Australia and New Zealand, who normally stay longer in this country, spent on average £158 and £200 respectively. The above expenditure included the cost of accommodation, meals, fares in this country, souvenirs and gifts. It excludes spending on large items such as cars and fares paid abroad by overseas visitors to UK carriers.

Taking into account both the number of visitors and expenditure per visitor, North America supplied in 1973 the biggest source of our tourist earnings, with 30 per cent of the total. 29 per cent came from EEC countries, 12 per cent from other west European countries and 29 per cent from the rest of the world. In 1974 the North American proportion fell slightly, reflecting the relative severity of the economic recession in the USA and higher air fares.

Holiday visitors to Britain in 1974 accounted for some 47 per cent of the total while 21 per cent came on business, 18 per cent stayed with friends and relatives and 14 per cent came for miscellaneous reasons including attendance at sporting events or for health or religious purposes ...

'Travel and tourism', *Economic Progress Report*, 66, September 1975.

## 2.9 **The nationalised industries**

Large parts of the energy and transport sectors had been brought into public ownership by the Attlee government to improve their efficiency, give greater public control over the economy and enhance economic democracy. These goals remained largely unfulfilled, however, and by the late 1970s serious questions were being asked about the future of the nationalised industries.

*Principal findings*

... By any standards the nationalised industries occupy a central role in our economy. Together they account for more than a tenth of the national product and nearly a fifth of total fixed investment. The four largest employers in the country (after central government) are nationalised industries. As suppliers they occupy a dominant position in energy, communications, steel and transport. They account for about a third of all the plant and equipment bought by British industry and for several sectors of industry they are the sole domestic supplier ...

In current conditions in Britain the management of any large industrial concern is a complex and difficult business. Attitudes to the social role of companies are changing; the role of employees and trade unions in decision taking is now being widely debated; and under the combined impact of inflation and slow growth the economic environment in which industry operates has steadily deteriorated.

In the nationalised industries these problems are accentuated. Because they are not subject to the same market disciplines as the private sector there is more scope for argument about their proper role and objectives. As monopoly providers of certain basic services their policies are a legitimate subject for public concern. Their dominant role as employers in some parts of the country has social and political implications which cannot be ignored. And their dependence on government as shareholder, banker and paymaster permeates their entire operations ...

*Main problems*

[O]ur analysis ... points to a lack of understanding within the government machine of the problems of industrial management. In particular, successive governments have been reluctant to accept the importance of continuity and to recognise that in any large industrial organisation, whether in the public or private sector, some assurance of stable objectives and policies is a precondition of efficiency.

The difficulty of reconciling the different time scales of politicians and industrialists was mentioned to us time and again. The problem is a familiar one and there is no easy solution for it; but it cannot simply be brushed under the carpet. In all the main nationalised industries, plans for investment, technology and manpower have to be made for periods which extend well beyond the lifetime of a single Parliament. Until a framework is established within which management can plan with confidence, the nationalised industries will never operate at anything like their full potential.

At the same time one must recognise the realities of our political system. People who work in nationalised industries – and evidence suggests that this applies to trade unions as well as management – deeply resent certain kinds of government intervention, especially when it seems to be based on short-term political expediency. Having seen the damage which such intervention can do both to performance and morale we have great sympathy with this view. But the fact is that Ministers in Britain are continually subjected to short-term pressures from many quarters and an elected government often feels obliged to respond to such pressures ...

*The need for change*

The evidence we have accumulated points overwhelmingly to the need to base the nationalised industries' relationship with the government on three basic concepts – trust, continuity and accountability. The present structure of relationships has manifestly failed to provide these. The lack of any assurance that when objectives and strategies have been agreed they will remain unchanged for long discourages any sense of commitment. Confusion over the respective roles of Ministers, civil servants and management means that no one can be properly held accountable for performance; those who do well cannot prove it objectively and those who want alibis for their mistakes can find them without difficulty. This has led to widespread resentment, cynicism and loss of morale among the people most involved.

For this reason we reject the argument that all that is needed is to put more effort into making the existing system work. We accept that, with goodwill and intelligent human relationships, individuals can make almost any system work. But our studies have shown that the present system is ill fitted to withstand the strains and pressures which arise when the going is difficult; and that in many respects it acts as a positive deterrent to mutual understanding. We are convinced that a completely new approach is needed.

Sir Ronald McIntosh, 'Introduction and summary' to National Economic Development Office, *A Study of UK Nationalised Industries: Their Role in the Economy and Control in the Future*, London, 1976, pp. 7–10.

## 2.10 The international competitiveness of UK manufactured goods

The first paragraph sets the context admirably.

In recent years there have been large differences between countries in rates of inflation and, accompanying these, large movements in nominal exchange rates. There have also been differences in the growth of productivity. Each of these factors affects the ability of manufacturers in one country to compete – in domestic and in world markets – with manufacturers in other countries, and so the measurement of relative competitiveness has attracted great interest. However, it is difficult to estimate the net effect of changes in prices, exchange rates and productivity using a unique measure of competitiveness: there are rather a number of complementary measures, each with certain advantages and disadvantages ... This article examines some of the measures of competitiveness which are commonly used, and compares the recent figures for the UK for each of them.

There are two important points to bear in mind in looking at these measures. First, all of them relate to price or cost competitiveness: they do not take account of non-price factors, such as quality or delivery performance. These factors are undoubtedly an important aspect of a country's competitive position, but they cannot be quantified in a comprehensive way. And second, the measures of competitiveness discussed in this article illustrate changes compared to a base year (1970). They cannot measure whether the UK was competitive in an absolute sense at any particular time. For that a view would have to be taken about the level of competitiveness that was appropriate to the desired current account balance: this level might itself change over time, for instance as a result of changes in non-price competitiveness.

*Measures of price competitiveness*

There are three basic measures of price competitiveness – relative export prices, import prices and relative wholesale prices.

The first of these, *relative export prices*, is defined as the ratio of the export prices of UK manufactures to a weighted average of the export manufactures of the UK's main competitors expressed in a common currency. While this does seem a natural way to measure competitiveness, it suffers from some major limitations:

- it relates only to the relative prices of UK and competitors' exports: it does not take account of how profitable exporting is for UK companies at this price. There is some evidence that in recent years UK exporters have become more inclined to follow the price charged by their competitors in world markets. This carries the implication that changes in the exchange rate are more likely to affect profit margins than export prices;
- it relates only to exports, and so does not take account of competition in the UK home market between imports and domestic production;

• it measures competitiveness only in relation to the exports of the UK's competitors: it does not, therefore, take into account competition with their domestic production in their home markets;

• it measures each country's delivery prices and not quotations, and so does not take account of unsuccessful quotations for exports.

Of these limitations the third might be eased by calculating the ratio of UK export prices to some combination of other countries' export and wholesale prices: but the statistical and conceptual difficulties in this approach are considerable. The other limitations are all inherent in the nature of this measure, and could only be overcome by using a different measure of competitiveness ...

An alternative to measuring the competitiveness of our exports against those of other countries is to measure the competitiveness of home production against imports – *import price competitiveness*. A common measure used is the ratio of UK wholesale prices of manufactures to the price of imports of manufactures. This measure does provide a guide to import competitiveness, but it does not take account of the relative profitability of UK firms on their domestic sales and overseas exporters on their sales to the UK. The third measure of price competitiveness which has some attractions is the ratio of UK wholesale prices to a weighted average of competitors' wholesale prices of manufactures – *relative wholesale prices*. This measure compares prices in the UK domestic market with the prices with which UK exports will be competing in other countries' domestic markets, and conversely, compares prices in other countries' domestic markets with the prices with which their exports will be competing in the UK market. But it does perhaps shift too much emphasis on to the domestic markets.

An alternative is to look at *cost* competitiveness rather than the price competitiveness of exports or imports. This has several advantages:

• a cost indicator covers all manufacturing industries: those which are exporting, those which are potential exporters, and those who are facing competition from imports;

• a cost indicator is not affected by whether changes in costs are reflected in prices or in profit margins;

• a cost indicator would in principle relate better to quotations for exports, both in terms of the timing of the orders and the coverage of quotations accepted and rejected, than a series of export prices.

The main disadvantage of measures of cost competitiveness lie, in fact, in the problems of constructing a suitable index. Ideally, a measure of cost competitiveness should cover all costs, but in practice comparisons are inevitably restricted to labour costs, because of the lack of suitable data elsewhere. Labour costs, incidentally, measure more than just wages and salaries: they include, for example, such costs as the employers' social security contributions. But obviously they do not take account of the costs of materials. How much this affects the results will depend upon how much costs of materials vary between manufacturers in different countries: it can be argued that they do not vary much, since the goods are homogeneous and the price is likely to be fixed internationally. If this is so, then movements in relative labour costs will be a good guide to movements in total costs, although they will tend to overstate them since labour costs represent only a part of total costs.

The labour costs of a manufacturer in one country relative to those in another are affected by movements in productivity, as well as by movements in wage rates or in exchange rates. For this reason, the appropriate measure to use in comparing costs is relative costs per unit of output. However, productivity and thus unit labour costs tend to vary cyclically with the level of capacity utilisation ... It is thus preferable to base the measure on 'normal' or 'cyclically adjusted' unit labour costs, even though this adjustment involves judgements about the trend levels of productivity and is not an easy one to make ...

*The competitive position of the UK*

The measures discussed in this article all have advantages and disadvantages and, for a complete view, movements in all of them should be studied. But if a single indicator is needed, then in most contexts *relative normal unit labour costs* probably provide the best measure ...

The table shows figures for the UK from 1970 for each of the four measures of competitiveness discussed. For each of these measures a *lower* value implies a more competitive position. Some of the more recent figures are estimates, since it takes some time for the data on countries' export prices and unit labour costs to become available ...

As is readily apparent from the table, the different measures show differing movements in competitiveness at various times. Of particular interest are the movements since thc beginning of 1976, when all four indices were fairly closely grouped together. In the course of 1976 all the measures showed substantial improvements in competitiveness as sterling fell: the improvements were most marked in the index of relative normal unit labour costs and the index of relative wholesale prices. In 1977 all the measures showed a deterioration in competitiveness relative to the levels reached at the end of 1976. The index of relative normal unit labour costs rose slightly, but is still at a historically low level. The other three indices showed fairly sharp rises (i.e. losses in competitiveness) in 1977, taking them back to, or above, the levels reached at the end of 1976. As was emphasised earlier, none of these measures can give an indication of whether UK industry is *absolutely* competitive at present: all they can show is competitiveness now *relative* to an earlier period. And as is clear from the figures, even the relative competitive position will depend upon which measure is considered appropriate.

'The international competitiveness of UK manufactured goods', *Economic Progress Report*, 95, February 1978.

**Measures of competitiveness of UK manufactured goods, 1970 = 100**

| | *Relative export prices* | *Import price competitiveness* | *Relative wholesale prices* | *Relative normal unit labour costs* |
|---|---|---|---|---|
| 1970 | 100.0 | 100.0 | 100.0 | 100.0 |
| 1971 | 102.2 | 104.2 | 106.9 | 103.1 |
| 1972 | 102.6 | 104.8 | 105.5 | 100.8 |
| 1973 | 94.1 | 98.5 | 90.8 | 91.8 |
| 1974 | 93.1 | 103.6 | 90.2 | 97.9 |
| 1975 | 96.5 | 103.7 | 98.5 | 99.2 |
| 1976 1st qtr | 99.2 | 100.8 | 99.2 | 99.0 |
| 2nd qtr | 94.4 | 95.1 | 91.6 | 91.8 |
| 3rd qtr | 95.0 | 93.7 | 90.4 | 90.1 |
| 4th qtr | 90.4 | 90.9 | 86.0 | 82.4 |
| 1977 1st qtr | 95.5 | 96.4 | 92.4 | 85.1 |
| 2nd qtr | 97.7 | 98.3 | 94.0 | 85.2 |
| 3rd qtr | 99.9 | 101.1 | 96.1 | 84.7 |
| 4th qtr | 104.1 | 103.8 | 99.1 | 88.3 |

## 2.11 The challenge of microelectronics

One of the reasons for the very rapid pace of technological change throughout the world since 1945 has been the development of new technologies, such as electronics, and their diffusion into many parts of the manufacturing and service sectors.

*Microelectronics – what is it?*

The term 'microelectronics' applies to electronic components or circuits of very small dimensions. There are a number of kinds of microelectronic device, but the best known – and the cornerstone of the present microelectronics industry – is the silicon integrated circuit (SIC). A SIC is produced by creating a succession of very thin layers of metal and component material on a silicon wafer, using a series of photographic masks to achieve the desired pattern of electronic components and interconnections in the microcircuit. The technique has been developed to the point where thousands of individual circuit components can be formed into a single microcircuit 'chip' measuring about $\frac{1}{4}$ inch square. Microelectronic technology now makes possible the production of cheap, reliable and compact electronic devices with a performance that has hitherto only been available from bulky and expensive mainframe computers – hence its importance. The new devices can be used to replace – and improve – the mechanical and electrical control systems in a wide range of existing products and processes, and also to create wholly new products. They are likely to find uses in a very wide range of industries and services; indeed it is difficult to think of any sector of industry which may not eventually be affected.

*The effects*

The advent of microelectronics tends to be regarded with a mixture of hope and fear. The hopes focus on the possibilities which will be opened up for new and improved products, cleaner and safer production methods and hence better working conditions, improved public services, especially in fields like medical diagnosis and treatment and education, and so on ...

The fears centre mainly on the impact on employment. There have been gloomy predictions from some quarters of industries collapsing and unemployment rising as microelectronics are introduced. The government recognises these fears, which are natural, particularly at a time of high unemployment, but believes that they should be put in perspective. Three points need to be emphasised: the change, though possibly great, will not happen overnight; jobs will be created as well as displaced; and, in a competitive world trading environment, failure to apply the new technology in the UK is much more likely to be damaging to employment than a positive response.

So far as the first point is concerned, the rate at which the effects come through will differ between sectors – for example, those sectors directly subject to foreign competition may well need to respond particularly quickly. The impact on the economy and total employment will therefore be staggered.

The second point – that there will be job gains as well as job losses – is based upon previous experience that those sectors and indeed countries that have had the best record of innovation or productivity growth have also achieved the highest growth in employment and output. There is no reason to doubt that this could be the case with microelectronics.

In both manufacturing industry and services there will be job losses due to higher productivity or the outdating of existing products; and in some cases these effects will be substantial and occasionally rapid. But against this, jobs will be created in the production of silicon chips and in software systems and applications. Early replacement of plant and machinery with new equipment incorporating microelectronics will create extra jobs in the capital goods industries provided that they can beat the competition from imports. There will also be job creation effects where microelectronics make possible entirely new products. Looking at the overall effect on the economy, the reduction in prices and the higher earnings in industries which apply the new technology will tend to increase overall demand at home, but any fall in employment in other industries will have an offsetting effect ...

It is of course difficult to make quantitative predictions of the balance between job-creating and job displacing effects. These will obviously depend on the speed of change, the willingness of industry to invest in the new technology and of people to acquire new skills and to change jobs, and the intensity of overseas competition. However ... claims that microelectronics will lead to higher unemployment should be treated sceptically.

What is certain, and this is the third point mentioned above, is that our major competitors in world markets are responding to the opportunities presented by microelectronics. If we do not keep up in the race we shall not only fail to obtain our share of the additional output, employment and wealth which the new technology offers, but will see our existing industry undermined by competition from new products produced elsewhere in the world. Substantially more jobs are at risk through loss of markets than through productivity increases.

*Economic Progress Report*, 107, February 1979.

## 2.12 North Sea contribution to GNP

Reserves of oil and gas were discovered in the British sector of the North Sea in the 1960s, and oil began to flow in 1975. The flow of oil and gas grew very rapidly, and began to make a major contribution to GNP. However, North Sea oil and gas were not an unqualified gain for the economy, as the final paragraph hints.

The projections [of future oil production] make the working assumption that the future real world price of oil remains constant ... and that the level of oil production will be consistent with the revised ranges recently published ... these ranges are set out in Table 1.

***Table 1*** **Forecast of oil production** (million tons)

| | |
|---|---|
| 1980 | 80–5 |
| 1981 | 85–105 |
| 1982 | 90–120 |
| 1983 | 95–130 |
| 1984 | 95–135 |

*Contribution to GNP*

Estimates of the direct contribution of oil and gas to GNP are set out in Table [2] ... The direct contribution to GNP is defined as the total sales value of oil and gas production less the goods and services bought in from outside the North Sea sector and less the interest profits and dividends due abroad. The contribution in 1979 was a little over 2 per cent of GNP. By 1983 it may rise to around 4.25 per cent of GNP. While this represents a significant proportion of GNP it is less than the contribution from, say, construction or agriculture and food production.

***Table* 2 Direct contribution of oil and gas production to GNP** (£ billion at 1978–79 prices)

| | *1978* | *1979* | *1980* | *1981* | *1982* | *1983* |
|---|---|---|---|---|---|---|
| Value of oil and gas production | 3.4 | 5.5 | 7.4 | 8.3 | 9.0 | 9.7 |
| *less* goods and services bought outside the sector | 0.5 | 0.6 | 0.7 | 0.7 | 0.8 | 0.9 |
| *less* interest profits and dividends due abroad | 0.6 | 1.3 | 1.7 | 1.8 | 1.5 | 1.6 |
| Contribution to GNP | 2.3 | 3.6 | 5.0 | 5.8 | 6.7 | 7.2 |
| as percent of GNP in that year | 1.25 | 2.25 | 3.00 | 4.00 | 4.00 | 4.25 |

The direct contribution of oil and gas to GNP does not measure the extent to which GNP is higher as a result of oil and gas production. For example, some of the direct contribution might be offset initially at least by lower output from some other sectors than might otherwise have been achieved.

*The effect of higher oil prices*

Higher world oil prices, if matched by higher North Sea oil prices, ... will ... raise the contribution of the North Sea to GNP; but it will not necessarily mean that the UK is better off in absolute terms overall. The UK is likely to be at most a small net exporter of oil in the 1980s, and so, unlike the major oil exporters, would not extract more than a small net increase in income from other countries when oil prices rise. To offset this increase part of the increased value of North Sea oil production accrues to foreign oil companies and is reflected in higher interest, profits and dividends due abroad. At the same time sharp increases in oil prices are disruptive to the world economy and hence likely to have an adverse effect on non-oil sectors of the UK economy.

*Economic Progress Report*, 123, July 1980.

## 2.13 The outlook for the British chemical industry from 1983 to 1991

Chemicals were justly regarded as one of Britain's more internationally competitive industries in the early 1980s. The report divided the industry into three – static, growth and problem sectors. The static sector comprised four small but mature parts of the industry (agrochemicals, dyestuffs and pigments, paints, soaps and detergents) which together accounted for approximately 15 per cent of the output of the British chemical industry.

### Sectors with above-average prospects

*Pharmaceuticals*

At present, nearly 80 per cent of world consumption of pharmaceuticals is in the developed countries, and this proportion is unlikely to change significantly. The USA and Japan are the largest single markets: the UK is sixth, taking only 4 per cent of world production. The UK has held its place among the 'big five' pharmaceutical exporting countries and is the home of about 11 per cent of world R&D.[18]

Continuation of the UK's pattern of relative strength and success through the 1980s may be jeopardised by factors which are outside the industry's control.

The first of these affects innovation, where there will continue to be important areas for development and potential major success. But these opportunities will be as visible and as keenly pursued in other countries with strong pharmaceutical industries. Research and development are expensive and long-term, and testing requirements are becoming steadily more protracted and stringent. Reductions in government research funding now threaten the national 'research base' in universities and hospitals and the clinical testing of new drugs in hospitals is becoming more difficult ...

The second area of risk is government health-care budgets and policies, where governments in general may be expected to continue to limit expenditure on drugs by various means. Some such measures can be positively harmful to the position and prospects of the UK pharmaceutical industry, and should therefore be avoided.

Pharmaceuticals at present account for 12 per cent of UK chemical industry turnover, 11 per cent of exports and 6 per cent of imports. The sector has the potential to make a larger contribution to the industry's overall performance.

*Specialised organics*
The ... specialised organics sector accounted for 6 per cent of UK chemicals output in 1980. The UK has about 7 per cent of world trade by value.

World demand is expected to keep pace with the growth of industrial and economic activity – which is not expected to be high. Additional opportunities will come from the expansion or diversification of existing customers, the development in new countries of existing customer industries and the appearance of quite new customers, applications and industries: they may be dramatic but cannot be predicted and will probably not generate much volume demand for some time. New competitors (in NICs[19] or the developed countries, including Japan in particular) are expected and opportunities will be equally visible to alert firms anywhere. In short, there will be opportunities for growth in a growing market but increasingly fierce competition.

The UK industry (about seventy firms of different sizes and degrees of involvement) did well in the late 1970s and turned its trade deficit into a surplus ...

**Sectors facing severe problems**

*Fertilisers*
Fertilisers account for about 18 per cent of the world chemicals industry's output and 5 per cent of the UK industry's sales.

Demand will continue to grow strongly, albeit at rates lower than those achieved in the 1970s, as overall world economic growth slows. The deceleration will be most marked in the developed countries.

Raw materials are, in most cases, controlled by a small number of producer countries which determine prices.

The relatively low value per tonne of fertilisers means that ability to compete has strong geographical limits.

Production costs largely depend upon raw material costs, which may depend upon suppliers' pricing policies or simply on commercial negotiations. Differential pricing of phosphate rock by US producers has damaged the European industry and ammonia production has been boosted in the USSR and OPEC countries[20] by cheap gas which has little alternative use and which in OPEC would otherwise be flared. In addition, much of the world industry is now state-owned and not necessarily subject to the disciplines of profit and return on capital; the only relatively secure position for private producers is to achieve lower costs.

The western European market has considerable overcapacity and faces the threat from the USSR and OPEC: it does not offer a realistic market to UK producers.

The UK is not well placed: almost without exception producers with full control of plentiful raw materials are closer to the market than is the UK. The costs of shipping finished fertiliser to the UK and low production costs arising from higher UK capacity utilisation only partly offset the UK's current cost disadvantage.

The UK's main asset in fertiliser production is its gas reserves for ammonia. The world ammonia price will increasingly be set by the OPEC countries whose natural gas has little alternative value, and by the USSR, with almost half the world's reserves ... New plant investment for export in the UK would be viable only if OPEC and USSR price levels could be met ...

*Inorganics*

Though the total number of products is very large, the inorganics sector's output is dominated by a small number of low value-added, low unit-price, very large tonnage commodities. They are expensive to transport and production therefore tends to be close to markets and based on indigenous raw materials. Most products are energy-intensive, and about two-thirds of output goes to other sectors of the chemical industry.

Over the next few decades there will be a continuation of the shift of the centre of gravity of production to the mineral-rich and fast-growth economies. By 1991, however, the US and western European industries will still remain the largest, although importing their raw materials at a higher stage of chemical processing. No fundamental technological developments are foreseen, and improvements in production processes will be evolutionary, aimed particularly at energy efficiency ...

In the UK, the sector's dependence on domestic industry for about 70 per cent of its sales is worrying because of the uncertain prospects for the economy as a whole and the below average prospects of some consumer sectors such as paper, glass and fertilisers ...

*Petrochemicals*

Petrochemicals, which covers the large-scale production of commodity organic chemicals, plastics materials and synthetic rubbers, represents about 15 per cent of world chemical tonnage and about 30 per cent by value of UK chemicals output. International trade represents about 20 per cent of the sector's output. World production grew at about 5 per cent p.a. between 1970 and 1979. Almost 90 per cent of production in 1979 was in OECD countries. There was some movement away from these countries in the 1970s. The petrochemicals sector is currently undergoing a major structural change as supply capacity is brought more closely into line with demand ...

The UK industry has taken major steps towards rationalisation through reducing fixed costs, raising productivity, closing the less competitive plants and concentrating technical effort to improve the efficiency of the remaining plants. In this it has been considerably in advance of western European competitors. However, unless continental over-capacity is reduced it is by no means certain that the remaining UK operations will be able to sell enough of their product to satisfy operating rates and adequate profitability.

Chemicals Economic Development Committee, *Chemicals Industry: Report to the National Economic Development Council*, London, 1983, pp. 8–14.

## 2.14 London as an international financial centre

Growing concern about Britain's long-term ability to compete in world markets for manufactured goods led some, notably in the Treasury during the mid–1980s, to see financial services as a key to Britain's competitive survival.

*London as an international financial centre*

As an international financial centre London ranks in the top three with New York and Tokyo. Despite the rise of new competitors, the UK has retained a leading role in the international banking markets, particularly in eurocurrency[21] activity. The world's largest 100 banks are all represented in London ... The stock exchange, however, no longer ranks among the largest in the world. In terms of turnover, it is in fifth position, far behind New York, Tokyo,

NASDAQ (the American electronic over-the-counter system) and just behind the German exchanges. In terms of market capitalisation of domestic shares, it is the third largest. An impressive number of overseas equities are also listed on the London stock exchange: traditionally active trading in non-UK securities has taken place mainly outside the exchange, though this is likely to change in consequence of the regulatory structure which is in the process of being set up.

Without the euromarkets, i.e. markets for deposits, loans and securities held outside their country of origin, London might have lost its position as a leading financial centre. These markets, initially almost exclusively in dollars, were made possible in the late 1950s when several countries decided to make their currencies freely convertible for non-residents. Encouraged by large external deficits and the imposition of regulations in the USA in the 1960s, they were given a further boost in the 1970s by the large balances accumulated by the OPEC countries following the oil price rise. London was the favoured location for the recycling of oil funds after the two oil shocks ... [I]t was mainly the combined effect of London's historic importance and a regulatory environment sympathetic to the pursuit of international banking which made it the largest centre of the euromarkets; other factors include the concentration of a full range of financial services in a very small area, the standard of supporting services, and time zone advantages. In order to maintain the UK's leading position in world financial markets, the authorities have pursued a consistent policy of market liberalisation, removing exchange controls and encouraging foreign banks and institutions to locate in London.

The number of foreign-owned banks ... in London rose from about 100 in the mid–1960s to almost 500 at the end of 1985, significantly exceeding the number of British-owned banks in the UK. About 120 foreign securities houses are established in the City ... In late 1985, almost 40 per cent of Japanese-owned banks' international business was accounted for by their London branches and subsidiaries, and the scale of international business conducted by Japanese banks in London approached that of all banks in Japan. Foreign banks (including consortium banks) account for about 80 per cent of all international bank lending in London, slightly more than ten years ago. The foreign banks have also turned their attention to the UK domestic markets ...

Although London has remained a leading financial centre, its dominant position has been gradually eroded ... [a]s the UK's share of world exports of financial services has declined since the 1960s, though at a slower pace in recent years. Its share of international bank lending has fallen from almost 30 per cent in the mid–1970s to below one-quarter, with a tendency to decrease again in recent years ...

Growth of overseas earnings in insurance and other brokerage has been lower than in banking. Anecdotal evidence suggests that insurance has been affected by protectionism abroad and the development of competing 'Lloyds type' insurance markets overseas. But the loss in market share has been most pronounced in securities trading. Over the last ten years turnover on the London stock exchange has grown at only half the rate achieved by the New York, Tokyo and German exchanges. As noted above, an important parallel market in eurobonds and, more recently, international equities has developed in London. But part of the market for international and UK shares has drifted overseas, in particular to New York where shares are traded ... at lower transaction costs.

Concerned with the UK securities industry's ability to compete in domestic and international markets, the authorities have encouraged structural change, including the removal of barriers to foreign entry into an exchange that was constituted as a private club. In the context of these reforms, which culminated in the 'big bang', the stock exchange has agreed ... to establish a single international and domestic equity market ... this should enhance London's prospects as a major centre for trading international securities. The European Community's decision to gradually remove all barriers to capital movements will present substantial opportunities for the City, given its unparalleled expertise in financial services. However, the worldwide trend towards financial market liberalisation will tend to increase the relative attraction of other centres, all the more so as prudential controls have been tightened in the UK. Besides New York and Tokyo, London is the logical third leg in the world's emerging round-the-clock trading system. But the application of new information and communication technologies also weakens the case for the physical concentration of financial services. Nonetheless, the existing infrastructure together with the depth of the market and the wide range of instruments available should help to maintain London's position as a major financial centre.

*OECD Economic Surveys, 1986–87: United Kingdom*, Paris, 1987, pp. 37–40.

## 2.15 Britain's 'islands of manufacturing excellence'

This article sought to identify the strong parts of the British manufacturing sector and account for their strength.

Which are the UK's best companies? Most people would plump for the conspicuous competitors at international level: the drugs companies Glaxo, SmithKline Beecham and Wellcome; Unilever, GrandMet and Guinness in food and drink; oil companies Shell and BP; Rolls-Royce, which has 22 per cent of the savagely competitive world aero-engine market; parts of the automotive components suppliers such as Lucas, GKN and Smiths Industries; bits of ICI and Courtaulds in chemicals and paint; parts of BTR; and possibly British Steel.

But although Ministers never tire of boasting that Britain is well represented among the very biggest world firms, that is misleading. Below that level, the picture changes remarkably. Many of the UK's best companies aren't British at all. They are companies like Rank Xerox, IBM in Havant and Greenock, Compaq, NCR, Black and Decker, Philips, Kodak, Milliken (textiles), Mars and Pedigree Petfoods, Sony, Peugeot and Nissan, soon to be joined by Honda and Toyota – all of whose UK manufacturing plants are among the best in the world. To these can be added professed or *de facto* international joint ventures such as ICL-Fujitsu, Rover-Honda and GEC-Alsthom, the power-engineering group.

In all, foreign manufacturers have invested £40 billion in the UK in the last five years – and the influx is continuing. One recent estimate is that by the year 2000, one in five UK manufacturing jobs will be in foreign-owned plants. That could well be an underestimate as recession continues to hack away at the comparatively under-managed, under-resourced UK-owned firms .... It is these foreign-owned plants that are redefining the nature of the British industrial base and hauling it into the late twentieth century.[22] There may be no indigenous motor industry bar Rover and Rolls-Royce,[23] but courtesy of the transplants the UK will be a major car exporter by mid-decade. Shipbuilding, bikes, washing machines and cutlery have gone, but the country has a balance-of-trade surplus on television sets, thanks to Sony, Toshiba and Hitachi.

In Silicon Glen, the UK makes 40 per cent of Europe's desk-top computers. Whatever the travails of British Rail, through GEC-Alsthom, the UK surprisingly makes part of the French engineering flagship, the TGV. Without these plants, the employment and balance of payments prospects for British manufacturing would scarcely bear thinking about.

Now put these together with the indigenous British successes. As well as cars, computers and televisions, there are world-class plants, British manned and managed, turning out machine tools, power tools, automotive and TV components, textiles, construction equipment (JCB), hi-fi (Linn Products), copiers and automated teller machines, tinned foods, confectionery, soft drinks and much else besides.

All this disposes of some weighty bits of conventional wisdom ... [G]iven the proper tools there's nothing wrong with British plants that good methods can't cure. There isn't a cultural problem or a worker problem, just a management problem.

Beyond that, if British plants can successfully manufacture in all these areas, there's no prior reason why the UK shouldn't manufacture anything else it currently imports. Nor, contrary to what the government has assumed during the wasted 1990s, is there anything inevitable about the UK surrendering any part of its industrial base ...

But the facts also demand some explanation. If British-managed plants can do well, why does British ownership seem to be a handicap? Some answers emerge from a look at the characteristics of successful firms.

The first and most obvious feature of the excellent plants is stability of ownership and control. That is, they have a stable environment in which to plan and invest – essential when, for instance, it takes ten years to absorb and install the techniques which make up 'lean' or 'frugal' manufacturing.

In this context it is hardly surprising that the best British manufacturing plants belong to firms that are very large, foreign or private. Foreign firms, securely owned and controlled, have a different attitude to investment and innovation ... Good players ... are prepared to make long-term investment for strategic change.

But managers in British firms too often can't do that. It's not that there isn't money available. It's that top managers, driven by bonus schemes and fear of stock market reaction, set ludicrously short payback periods, effectively disqualifying all but short-term schemes for patching and cost-cutting ...

The second obvious feature of the UK's best plants is that they are outward-facing; in global industries, or at the least large-scale exporters. By definition, foreign-owned plants belong to international firms, which are most efficiently exposed to new product and process innovations, value new management ideas, and adopt them more quickly. International companies also attract the best managers and put more effort into training them ...

The third characteristic of excellence is at first sight counter-intuitive. The best and strongest firms congregate in the toughest, most competitive sectors, not those that give the easiest ride. Foreign-owned firms with their longer time horizons are less likely to shirk this uncomfortable but productive competition, while there is plenty of evidence ... that British-owned firms give up too easily.

Simon Caulkin, 'Manufacturing: dead but not buried', *The Guardian*, Saturday 27 March 1993.

## 2.16 Two decades of industrial stagnation, 1974–94

Amid increasing concern about the state of British manufacturing in the early 1990s, a leading economic commentator looks back on the previous forty years.

[Between 1954 and 1974] manufacturing output in the UK rose by a creditable – if, by European standards, unspectacular – 86 per cent. Twenty years ago the index of manufacturing output (1990 = 100) was standing at 96.3.

The latest figure, for April 1994, shows that it is now 97.9. That represents a total increase of 1.66 per cent during the last twenty years. In other words, a (crude) increase of only 0.083 per cent each year. We have ceased to be a serious manufacturing nation.

No, I haven't got the decimal point wrong. The country which invented the industrial revolution and which, during the 1980s, enjoyed unprecedented windfall revenues from North Sea oil and privatisation and which experienced an 'economic miracle' under Mrs Thatcher has managed to increase its manufacturing output by only a contemptible 0.083 per cent a year.

Of course, this may understate underlying output. Corporate 'downsizing' means some activities counted as manufacturing a decade ago (like catering and maintenance) are now contracted out to firms in the service industries. It is also possible that statisticians haven't adjusted properly for the output of products like computers whose prices have been falling rapidly.

But no special pleading will turn a disaster into a success. Nor will it affect comparisons with other countries because their statistics are susceptible to similar revisions. OECD figures show that between 1970 and 1989 (that is, excluding the latest recession, but including the strong 11.5 per cent rise in 1971–73) UK manufacturing output rose by 21 per cent. And elsewhere? Manufacturing output in Italy rose by 60 per cent, in France by 47 per cent, in the USA by 92 per cent, in Japan by 118 per cent and in Ireland by 202 per cent.

What can be done? Even at this late stage there ought to be agreement by all warring factions on one simple point. The argument shouldn't be over whether manufacturing is uniquely important or whether it doesn't matter at all, but that we as a nation surely, surely, have the ability to do a bit better than a pathetic rise of 0.08 per cent a year.

Victor Keegan, 'Special pleading cannot hide UK's industrial failure', *The Guardian*, Monday 27 June 1994.

## 2.17 The decline of manufacturing: an alternative view

It is possible to view the relative decline of manufacturing in a different light, as a trend common to almost all developed countries, the dangers of which have been exaggerated – as below.

Does it matter that manufacturing provides fewer people with their livelihoods? Many believe that it does: they see it as both a cause and symptom of more general economic decline.

The 'manufacturing matters' school claims that manufacturing jobs are superior to service jobs in several ways ...

*Productivity*

Consider the argument that service jobs are less productive than manufacturing jobs and that productivity grows more slowly in services than in manufacturing ...

Official statistics do indeed show that productivity rises more slowly in service industries than in manufacturing. Real output per employee in manufacturing grew by an average of 3.1 per cent a year in the seven biggest OECD economies between 1979 and 1990; in services, productivity increased at a measly annual rate of 0.9 per cent. But it is hard to judge how accurate such figures are. Many economists reckon that statisticians consistently underestimate the rate of growth of service sector productivity.[24]

*Wages and skills*

Another common belief is that workers are paid less in service-sector jobs than in manufacturing ...

It is true that pay rates in manufacturing are often higher than in services. The average hourly pay of an American manufacturing worker in 1993 was $11.75; workers in retail trade got a paltry $7.29. But workers in finance ($11.32) and in wholesale trade ($11.71) came closer to their metal-bashing brethren. And service industries are catching up: pay increases in wholesaling and finance have outstripped those in manufacturing over the past decade.

Moreover, comparisons are made trickier by the huge range of service-sector jobs: the classification 'business services' alone covers everything from cleaning to consultancy. There are certainly many poorly paid, low-skilled jobs in services. But an increasing proportion of service workers are highly skilled; and their skills are based on knowledge. Designers, accountants and bankers fall into this group ...

*Technology*

Some people claim that technological change happens mainly in manufacturing industries ... Service industries, it is sometimes suggested, cannot exploit new technology to drive the economy forward.

In fact, many services have become increasingly high-tech. Firms in the world's increasingly interconnected and complex financial markets need ever more sophisticated computer programmes. The telecommunications and entertainment industries are going digital at breathtaking speed. The rapidly growing health-care business calls for increasingly sophisticated medical and pharmaceutical research.

*Trade*

Services are often said to have a lower export content than do manufacturing industries ...

Although some services – such as hairdressing and road sweeping – cannot be exported, many others can. Trade in services is becoming increasingly important: services' share of world trade rose from 17 per cent in 1980 to 22 per cent in 1992. Around a quarter of America's exports are services. Tourism alone contributes 7 per cent.

**So where's the problem?**

There is a more fundamental reason why the shift of employment from manufacturing to services is less worrying than some economists and politicians claim. The conventional division between manufacturing and services is based on a misconception of how economies now work.

Changes in manufacturing and service businesses have blurred the distinction between the two. So much so, indeed, that it may now be of little use. Manufacturers have come to rely on services for a greater proportion of their inputs. Cars, computers and hi-fis are not merely manufactured – they are also designed, marketed, advertised and distributed. A significant and rising part of the value added by manufacturers now consists of services.

The decline of manufacturing employment and the rise of service-sector jobs is also a consequence of the way manufacturing companies are organised. Most manufacturing firms used to provide a wide range of services in-house. They employed their own accountants, cleaners and cooks. These days, however, they are much more likely to buy in auditing, cleaning, catering and other business services from specialised service companies. Some of the shift from manufacturing to service employment is therefore a statistical illusion.

*The Economist*, 19 March 1994.

# 3
# The balance of payments

After the growth rate, the balance of payments has been the most frequently used yardstick to judge post-war economic performance. In this area, relative decline is easy to identify, in the fall of the rate of exchange between the pound sterling and the currencies of Britain's main competitors. Governments have tried a wide range of initiatives to reverse the slide but without notable success. The story begins with wartime deterioration in Britain's external position.

## 3.1 Britain's wartime 'financial Dunkirk'

The coming to power of the Churchill coalition in 1940 had brought a new attitude to Britain's war effort; the government proposed to ignore the financial and foreign exchange costs and wage war to the utmost. US aid prevented wartime bankruptcy but when Treasury officials, led by Lord Keynes, came to look at the post-war balance of payments the picture was bleak indeed.

*Our overseas financial prospects*

Three sources of financial assistance have made it possible for us to mobilise our domestic manpower for war with an intensity not approached elsewhere, and to spend cash abroad, mainly in India and the Middle East, on a scale not even equalled by the Americans, *without having to export* in order to pay for the food and raw materials which we were using at home or to provide the cash we were spending abroad.

The fact that the distribution of effort between ourselves and our Allies has been of this character leaves us far worse off, when the sources of assistance dry up, than if the roles had been reversed. If we had been developing our exports so as to pay for our own current needs in addition to provide a large surplus which we could furnish free of current charge to our allies ... we should, of course find ourselves in a grand position when the period of providing the stuff free of current charge was brought suddenly to an end.

As it is, the more or less sudden drying up of these sources of assistance after the end of the Japanese war will put us in an almost desperate plight, unless some other source of temporary assistance can be found ... – a plight far worse than most people, even in government departments, have yet appreciated.

The three sources of finance have been (a) lend lease from the United States[1]; (b) mutual aid from Canada[2]; (c) credits (supplemented by sales of our pre-war capital assets) from the sterling area[3] (including credits under payments agreements with certain countries, especially in South America, which are outside the area, but have made special agreements with it).

In the present year, 1945, these sources are enabling us to overspend our own income at the rate of about £2,100 millions a year, made up roughly as follows ...

| | *£ million* |
|---|---|
| Lend lease (munitions) | 600 |
| Lend lease (non-munitions) | 500 |
| Canadian mutual aid | 250 |
| Sterling area, etc. | 750 |
| | 2,100 |

... How vividly do departments and Ministers realise that the gay and successful fashion in which we undertake liabilities all over the world and slop money out to the importunate represents an overplaying of our hand, the possibility of which will come to an end quite suddenly in the near future unless we obtain a new source of assistance? ...

We must ... allow for economies after VJ[4] in ... overseas expenditure for goods and for increased earnings from our shipping and from the expansion of our exports in 1946. To correct for these factors we have to embark on difficult guesswork, and the range of reasonable estimating is very wide.

In the cost of imports of food and raw materials an increase, rather than a reduction, is in sight, if the public are to be fed reasonably and employed fully and taking account of the fact that stocks are currently being drawn upon. We are budgeting (unless circumstances force us to restrict, as is quite possible) for more rather than less food in 1946 than in 1945. The raw materials required to provide employment, though not always the same in character as those we now import, are unlikely to be reduced in aggregate, since the numbers employed in industry will, after demobilisation, be more rather than less. On the other hand, some miscellaneous economies should be possible. One way and another our import programme might be kept down to £1,300 million. Even this, assuming prices at double pre-war, means considerable austerity ...

As for exports there seems a reasonable hope of increasing them from an aggregate of £350 million in 1945 to £600 million in 1946. Extreme energy and concentration on this objective should do better still. Net invisible income in 1946, allowing for some recovery in commercial shipping receipts, might be put at £50 million.

On the assumption of an export and import price level double pre-war, and no major changes in present policies, the position in 1946 can, therefore, be summed up as follows [see table].

| | *£ million* | | *£ million* |
|---|---|---|---|
| Imports | 1,300 | Exports | 600 |
| Government expenditure overseas | 450 | Net invisible income | 50 |
| | | Government receipts from Allies and Dominions | 150 |
| | | | 800 |
| | | Deficit | 950 |
| | 1,750 | | 1,750 |

When we come to subsequent years, we are in the realm of pure guesswork. If, to cheer ourselves up, we make bold to assume that by 1949 we have reached the goal of increasing the volume of exports by 50 per cent, the value of exports in that year, at double pre-war prices, would be £1,450 million. If we suppose further that we can keep the further growth of imports within very moderate limits, if we can steadily curtail government expenditure overseas and if we can steadily increase our net invisible income, we can produce the following pipe dream [see table], showing an eventual equilibrium in the fourth year after VJ, namely 1949.

*(£ million)*

| | *Imports* | *Government expenditure overseas* | *Total* | *Exports* | *Net invisible income* | *Total* | *Deficit* |
|---|---|---|---|---|---|---|---|
| 1947 | 1,400 | 250 | 1,650 | 1,000 | 100 | 1,100 | 550 |
| 1948 | 1,400 | 200 | 1,600 | 1,300 | 100 | 1,400 | 200 |
| 1949 | 1,450 | 150 | 1,600 | 1,450 | 100 | 1,600 | nil |

Combining the assumed deficits in 1947 and 1948 with the estimated deficit of £950 millions in 1946, we have a total deficit of £1,700 million for the three years taken together,

Where on earth is all this money to come from? Our gold and dollar reserves at the end of 1945 will stand at about £500 million. We might, if necessary, draw on this to the tune of £250 million but certainly not more. In 1946 we might conceivably increase our net borrowing from the sterling area by (say) another £300 million ...

The conclusion is inescapable that there is no source from which we can raise sufficient funds to enable us to live and spend on the scale we contemplate except the United States ... It is sometimes suggested that we can avoid dependence on the United States by a system of semi-barter arrangements with the countries from which we buy. This, however, assumes that the limiting factor lies in the willingness of overseas markets to take our goods. Whatever may be the truth of this a few years hence, it will not be the position in the early post-war period which we have in view here. The limiting factor will be our physical capacity to develop a sufficient supply of export goods ...

It seems, then, that there are three essential conditions without which we have not a hope of escaping what might be described, without exaggeration and without implying that we should not eventually recover from it, a financial Dunkirk. These conditions are (a) intense concentration on the expansion of exports, (b) drastic and immediate economies in our overseas expenditure, and (c) substantial aid from the United States on terms which we can accept. They can only be fulfilled by a combination of the greatest enterprise, ruthlessness and tact.

J. M. Keynes, 'The present overseas financial position of the UK', memorandum dated 13 August 1945, reproduced in *The Collected Writings of John Maynard Keynes, 24: The Transition to Peace*, London, 1979. pp. 398–410.

## 3.2 Policy towards Europe after the war

This minute, written by a relatively junior but highly influential Treasury official, R.W. B. Clarke, records a discussion of senior Whitehall officials on policy towards Europe.

1. Since post-war planning began, our policy has been to secure close political, military and economic co-operation with USA. This has been necessary to get economic aid. It will always be decisive for our security.

2. The means to this is now the Atlantic Pact.[5] We hope to secure a special relationship with USA and Canada within this, for in the last resort we cannot rely upon the European countries. Although we may maintain a special relationship in fact, this will not be overtly recognised (at any rate while we are still a claimant for US economic aid). However, we must in practice establish the position that USA will defend us, whatever happens to the Europeans.

3. In order to get US aid, we have had to accept certain US concepts (e.g. ITO[6] and convertibility[7]). Our policy has been to work these out in good faith, and to abandon them only when it is clear to the Americans that we are forced to do so by hard facts and not duplicity. This policy is sound.

4. Under US pressure, and as a condition of ERP[8], we are pledged to European economic co-operation in OEEC.[9] We must seek to make OEEC a success; if it fails, we must show clearly to the Americans that this is not our fault.

5. On merits, there is no attraction for us in long-term economic co-operation with Europe. At best, it will be a drain on our resources. At worst, it will seriously damage our economy.

6. Economic co-operation in a structural sense (e.g. Customs Unions,[10] integration in extreme forms) is impossible without political federation. This must be ruled out of practical consideration.

7. But economic co-operation in this sense is irrelevant to European economic recovery. Its results could not appear for many years.

8. We have a major interest in European *recovery*. Failure of Europe to recovery [*sic*] spells communism. The Atlantic Pact is hopeless unless France, Benelux, etc., secure economic stability.

9. At the same time, it is doubtful whether the European countries *can* recover – i.e. can be independent of US aid by 1952 at the standard of living which is necessary to maintain social stability. This means that we must secure a *de facto* special relationship with USA. And that we must not burn our boats in Europe.

10. Our policy should be to assist Europe to recover as far as we can. We should be prepared to assist the Europeans to earn sterling; we should be prepared to let them have supplies. But the concept must be one of limited liability. In no circumstances must we assist them beyond the point at which the assistance leaves us too weak to be a worthwhile ally for USA if Europe collapses – i.e. beyond the point at which our own viability was impaired. For example, we should not be prepared to provide them with dollars (except where this suited us in our own interests). Nor can we embark upon measures of 'co-operation' which surrender our sovereignty and which lead us down paths along which there is no return.

11. OEEC will break down (and with it the whole ERP programme) unless we continue to take the lead. Discussion in OEEC is now becoming sterile and effective activity will break down unless a new idea is injected. If OEEC is to break down, the breakdown should be made to come because the other countries have rejected a clear, definite and reasonable lead from us. This is necessary for our relations with USA – in particular to prevent us from being written off as a failure alongside the other countries.

12. We should therefore accept the idea of M. Spaak[11] that we should put forward a European plan. We should advance this as a plan for European recovery, and not as a plan for long-term co-operation.

Minute of a meeting held on 5 January 1949, reproduced in Sir Richard Clarke, *Anglo-American Economic Collaboration in War and Peace* (ed. Sir Alec Cairncross), Oxford, 1982, pp. 208–9.

## 3.3 The balance of payments in the 1950s

This extract from the Radcliffe Committee's investigation into the working of the monetary system outlines the main developments in the balance of payments after 1947 and hints, in its last paragraph, at the problems of 'stop-go' – the need to restrict the growth of output to support the balance of payments.

Once the formidable task of bringing exports and imports into balance with each other had been achieved, it was possible to view the external situation with rather less anxiety. The balance of payments, though never very favourable, was rarely adverse after 1947. At no time was it necessary seriously to restrict the level of activity because of an adverse balance of payments, although some restriction might well have become necessary in the absence of American aid. All this contrasted strikingly with experience between the wars. There was, moreover, far less preoccupation with the competitive position of British exports ...

It was also possible after the war to make use of international financial institutions that did not exist before the war: the International Monetary Fund and the European Payments Union[12] were able to inject additional liquidity into the system and to provide stand-by credits of effect payments settlements, so relieving the strain on national reserves. International economic co-operation was also a great deal closer; the United States, as the most important creditor country, not only furnished help through international institutions but also accepted some direct responsibility for maintaining equilibrium in international payments.

The United Kingdom's position, in spite of high exports and international aid, was nevertheless an extremely precarious one. Large overseas debts had accumulated during and after the war; and on short-term account the country's sterling liabilities greatly exceeded her reserves of gold and foreign exchange, which were dangerously low. Moreover, although the balance of payments usually showed a surplus, it was inadequate to provide the capital which Commonwealth and other countries wished to borrow in London and at the same time build up a larger reserve. Whenever confidence in the pound fell low, or whenever the balance of payments became temporarily adverse, the drain on the reserves quickly reached danger point.

*Committee on the Working of the Monetary System, Report*, London, 1959 (Cmnd 827), pp. 10–11.

## 3.4 The Kennedy round of GATT

Under the General Agreement on Tariffs and Trade (GATT) protective barriers to trade were removed in stages throughout the post-war period. Each phased reduction in tariff levels had to be agreed in long-lasting, frequently difficult negotiating 'rounds'. The 'Kennedy round', completed in 1967, brought the largest reductions of tariff levels on trade in industrial goods.

At midnight last Monday agreement was reached in the Kennedy round. Trade covered by its tariff cuts approached $40 billion a year – mostly between the industrialised countries of the world; the tariff cuts themselves, to be spread over the next five years, average out on a simple arithmetical basis at something like one-third. These tower above anything achieved in the other worthy, but more limited, tariff-cutting conferences held since the war. The bargain means that Britain's tariffs on semi-manufactures will come down from 15 to 12 per cent; on manufactures from a present range of 10–33 per cent to 7.5 to 20 per cent. Britain's average tariffs remain higher than those of her main trading partners: ... about 5 per cent higher than the Common Market's on a very rough average, but only fractionally higher than America's. But all levels have fallen to the point where the bulk of tariffs on most (not all) industrial goods should now cease to count as formidable barriers to sales across frontiers. This is very roughly all we know for sure. Details of cuts on individual goods will dribble out in the next six weeks (so will details of concessions that won't be made) ...

The Kennedy round has ended far from its original commitment, but it surprised even the optimists of recent months by the depths of its final cuts. Even when the full details are known ... it will still be impossible to quantify the economic effects of the cuts. The Americans say they have spent three years and the lives of two computers in an abortive methodological attempt to chart the impact of tariffs – and of tariff cutting – on trade. Only the progressive implementation of tariff reductions in five annual stages starting next year will actually show the countries what they did at Geneva. But they have done something very worthwhile as between the main industrial countries.

Snags remain. Concessions to the underdeveloped world are no more than apologetic, although time just remains for bilateral deals to improve the package here a little.

*The Economist*, 20 May 1967.

## 3.5 **Devaluation in 1967**

The Attlee government had been forced to devalue in 1949 (from £1 = $4.03 to £1 = $2.80) and during the 1950s major balance of payments problems were avoided, as extract 3.3 indicates. But in the 1960s sterling again came under pressure. The Labour government which came to power in 1964 was committed to the prevailing exchange rate, but it too was forced into devaluation and, despite the Prime Minister's initial resolution, ultimately to sacrifice his growth strategy and into severely deflationary policies to make devaluation (to £1 = $2.40 – and not to a floating rate) effective.

On Saturday 4 November [1967] the Chancellor came to see me about sterling. The situation had suddenly worsened and following widespread rumours on the Continent that we should devalue in mid-November the drain on the reserves had intensified ... For the first time [Chancellor of the Exchequer] Jim Callaghan doubted whether we should be able to hold the position and for the first time I had the same doubts. I was anxious that there should be no repetition of the 1966 situation, with lobbying and intrigue on the policy and a feeling among Ministers that major decisions were being taken by too small a group of their colleagues. Over the weekend I decided to put the position on the record. I made clear that if the situation worsened, if the Chancellor were to feel that the alternatives to devaluation were unacceptable, I should accept his advice. There would be no question of what had been called a 'political veto'.[13] I warned him, however, that, apart from certain inevitable measures to constrain home consumption, I should be opposed to a major lurch into deflation. On the operational side, either devaluation or a decision to float the pound sterling would be disastrous if our action was followed, voluntarily or involuntarily, by too many others.[14] On the technique of devaluation, I favoured floating rather than a cut to a lower fixed parity.

Harold Wilson, *The Labour Government, 1964–70*, Harmondsworth, 1974, pp. 570–1.

## 3.6 Britain's 'invisible' earnings

As might be expected from Chapter 2, Britain's balance of trade in goods (visible trade) was usually in deficit, even in the 1950s and 1960s, whereas the balance of trade in services (invisible trade) was usually in surplus. This extract reviews the position in 1970.

More than £1 in every £3 Britain earns from abroad comes from 'invisible' transactions – mainly earnings from services such as transport, tourism, banking and insurance, and the interest received from investments overseas. Further, while our 'net' trade in goods – the difference between the value of 'visible' exports and imports – has usually been in deficit (by a comparatively small amount in relation to total trade), our 'invisible' earnings have usually exceeded our 'invisible' payments abroad. In 1969 and the first half of 1970 the invisible surplus was very large ...

*Composition and growth*

... The most noticeable features are the large excess of credits over debits in 'other services' and the interest, profits and dividends of the private sector. On the other hand, in the accounts for government services and for interest, profits and dividends for the public sector as a whole, payments exceeded receipts.

*Transport*

Shipping is the biggest single earner (in gross earnings) among our 'invisible' industries, although the balance on shipping transactions, while in surplus since 1967, is still comparatively small ... British airlines' overseas earnings rose strongly in 1969 [and] ... there was a net surplus on civil aviation of £41 million in 1969.

*Travel*

The travel account estimates the money which visitors to Britain spend here and which British travellers spend abroad. The cost of sea and air travel on international routes and affecting the balance of payments goes into the transport accounts.

The travel balance has moved from a deficit of nearly £100 million in 1965 to a surplus of £35 million in 1970.

*Other services*

... '[O]ther services' provide very large and by far the most strongly growing surplus, totalling £520 million in 1969, almost double the surplus in 1965 ...

The largest part of this very diverse group is 'financial and allied services', such as banking, insurance, merchanting and brokerage, based to a very large extent on the City of London. The table shows that our overseas insurance earnings have grown nearly fourfold since 1966, while banking and brokerage have doubled their foreign income. The financial institutions have also contributed much to the increase in investment income (included in 'interest, profits and dividend') and to the growth of British capital assets overseas.

**Earnings from financial and allied services** (£ million)

| | *1966* | *1967* | *1968* | *1969* |
|---|---|---|---|---|
| Insurance | 39 | 75 | 117 | 150 |
| Banking | 22 | 24 | 34 | 46 |
| Merchanting | 26 | 26 | 28 | 34 |
| Brokerage etc. | 27 | 31 | 44 | 54 |
| Total | 114 | 156 | 223 | 284 |

Among other private services, fees and other earnings from construction work overseas by British firms brought £55 million in 1969, overseas journalists and students spent £54 million here and overseas governments and forces spent over £90 million on private services (e.g. embassy costs and diplomats' and forces' spending).

Royalties, copyright and agency fees, advertising, etc., netted a surplus of £23 million from total gross earnings of £174 million in 1969, and we earn a fair surplus (£15 million in 1969) on the production and rental of films and TV programmes.

*Interest, profits and dividends ('IPD')*
... On balance, devaluation, as well as the recent increase in overseas investment (over £600 million in 1969) has led to a strong increase in our overseas earnings. Overseas earnings in Britain have also been rising, but they fell back in 1969 because profits on overseas investments in Britain were depressed. Net British private earnings therefore rose strongly in 1969. Some of these earnings (and of overseas earnings here) are not sent home but reinvested overseas (or here) ...

*Government spending*
Government invisible debits in 1969 (apart from interest payments) consisted of £329 million on services, mainly the cost of troops and diplomatic services abroad, and £175 million on transfers, mainly grants to developing countries. Overseas payments to the British government for military and other services here amounted to £46 million.

Despite higher costs overseas (partly resulting from devaluation) the net government deficit has been held at around the 1967 level for 2.5 years.

*Economic Progress Report*, 9 November 1970.

## 3.7 **Floating in 1972**

In June 1972 Britain was once more forced to devalue, but by now the Bretton Woods system was near collapse, making international finance much more unpredictable and encouraging British policy-makers to float sterling rather than opting for a new pegged exchange rate. The size of speculative movements seemed to indicate that markets rather than governments took the ultimate decisions on the value of currencies.

The decision to float sterling on 23 June was taken after a loss of reserves of over £1,000 million in six working days. The speed with which the selling of sterling developed once again emphasised the increasing size and volatility of the movements of short-term funds which can be generated in the foreign exchange markets. Such large and rapid movements create difficult problems of monetary management in the many countries involved, and bring home the pressing need to seek solutions through reform of the international monetary mechanism and the establishment of a more stable system.

On this occasion, the loss of confidence in sterling reflected less the present position than expectations about the UK economy – the balance of payments surplus on current account, though heavily reduced in the first half of the year, was still running at an annual rate of some £300 million a year, a figure which would have been considered adequate by the standards of the last two decades. It was rather the implications of recent developments for the future UK balance of payments which led to the selling of sterling – in particular the course of movements in domestic wages and prices; the unsettled state of industrial relations; and the likelihood that imports would rise as the economy expanded. There had also been considerable talk about the prospects for the balance of payments and the need to take action on the exchange rate when it became apparent that a change was necessary.[15]

These influences were reflected in the subsequent decline in the floating sterling rate which had by the end of July produced a depreciation in relation to the parities established last December of 6.75 per cent. Such a depreciation has its own inflationary effects. The UK government has already declared its intentions of returning to a fixed parity for sterling as soon as practicable. The accomplishment of this, however, and the maintenance thereafter of stable conditions, will be easier if there can be more assured prospects at home than in recent years of marked and lasting moderation in the rate of growth in domestic costs and prices. It must be hoped that the tripartite talks now taking place between the government, the TUC and the CBI will help towards this.

'Commentary', *Bank of England Quarterly Bulletin*, 12, 1972, pp. 325–6.

## 3.8 Economic implications of EEC membership

From the early 1960s onwards, British governments had looked with envy at the growth rates achieved by member countries of the EEC. Two applications for membership were rejected by the French President, de Gaulle. A third, ultimately successful negotiation for entry was launched by the Conservative Prime Minister, Edward Heath, in June 1970.

*The economic case*

The central question here is how membership of the community would affect the structure of our economy and so the prosperity of our people. For many years we have faced similar problems: difficulties with the balance of payments, a disappointing record in industrial investment, and an inadequate rate of economic growth. The result is that we have begun to drop seriously behind other countries, and particularly the members of the community, in attaining a higher standard of living.

The government believe that membership would provide the most favourable opportunity for achieving the progress which we all desire. Studies made by the Confederation of British Industries show that this belief is shared by a substantial majority of British industry. Our entry would not, of course, of itself bring about some automatic improvement in our performance and it would involve us in costs as well as benefits ...

Gradual adoption of the common agricultural policy will stimulate British farm output and open community markets to our food exports, but at the same time will raise food prices in the UK and the cost of our food imports. The extent of this increase in food prices and import costs will naturally depend on the difference between community and world food prices. This difference has narrowed significantly in the last two or three years. But assuming a continuation of the present price gap and allowing for the likely changes in patterns of UK production and consumption, the additional cost to our balance of payments on account of food imports seems unlikely to amount to more than about £5 million in the first year, and £50 million a year by the end of the transitional period ...

The effects on British industry will stem principally from the creation of an enlarged European market by the removal of tariffs between the UK and the community countries, and, less importantly, from other tariff changes. The response of British industry will be broadly of two different kinds. First, there will be an immediate reaction of a British exporter to each annual reduction in the tariff on his exports to the community. This response will involve a decision whether, for example, to maintain his prices and so increase his profit margins, or reduce his prices and expand his sales. But secondly, and in the long run far more significant than this response to relatively small annual changes in tariffs, will be industry's decisions on how to take advantage by structural changes of the opportunities opened up by the creation at the end of the transitional period of a permanent, assured, and greatly enlarged market. Manufacturers will be operating in a 'domestic market' perhaps five times as large as at present, in which tariff barriers cannot be put up against them however well they do. There will in consequence be a radical change in planning, investment, production and sales effort.

Any calculation of the effects on the balance of trade of these tariff changes will only produce a valid estimate if it takes account of the parallel existence of both these influences operating on industry. And a simple summation of estimates of industry's immediate responses to the small annual tariff changes involved would reflect only the false assumption that no other changes were taking place. The government do not believe that the overall response of British industry to membership can be quantified in terms of its effect upon the balance of trade. They are confident that the effect will be positive and substantial, as it has been for the community.

*The United Kingdom and the European Communities*, London, 1971 (Cmnd 4715).

## 3.9 The IMF loan, 1976

In autumn 1976, Denis Healey, the Chancellor of the Exchequer in the Labour government, decided that the only way to restore market confidence in sterling was to seek financial support from the IMF, which meant agreeing policy targets with the IMF. He also had to persuade the Cabinet to accept the same targets. Both goals were achieved, but his reflections on the episode question whether the enormous disruption was economically and financially necessary.

Yet, in a sense, the whole affair was unnecessary. The Treasury had grossly overestimated the PSBR,[16] which would have fallen within the IMF's limit without any of the measures they prescribed. Later figures showed that we also managed to eliminate our current account deficit in 1977, before the IMF package had had time to influence it. Thus I was able to introduce a reflationary budget in 1978 to undo the damage done by excessive deflation in 1977 ... without infringing any of my undertakings to the IMF.

Moreover, I drew only half of the loan offered in return by the

IMF, and had repaid it all – or the equivalent – by the time I left office. Similarly, over half the stand-by credit remained untouched ... During the long agony of the IMF negotiations I used longingly to talk of 'Sod-off day' – the moment when I would at last be free of IMF control. 'Sod-off Day' came much earlier than anyone expected.

In practice, however, we could have done without the IMF loan only if we – and the world – had known the real facts at the time. But in 1976 our forecasts were far too pessimistic, and we were still describing our public expenditure in a way which was immensely damaging to our standing in the financial markets.

Another major factor in the impression of muddle we created was a fundamental disagreement, inside both the Treasury and the Bank of England, about economics in both theory and practice. This disagreement existed in many countries. It reflected the uncertainties created by the breakdown of the international economic order which had been created at the end of the war, largely by American and British experts under the influence of Keynes.

The core of this agreement concerned the role of exchange rates, and the techniques of controlling them. The Bretton Woods treaty required all governments to keep the value of their currencies fixed in relation to the dollar, changing their rates rarely, and only by mutual agreement ... Bretton Woods broke down when the Johnson government refused to continue carrying the special burdens it imposed on the United States.[17] A few years later, the increase in oil prices made a regime of floating currencies inevitable. In such a regime the value of a currency depended on the demand for it in the financial markets, which were not subject to control by any government.

Because at that time markets distrusted governments which were significantly in debt either at home or abroad, the deficits which Keynesian theory recommended when demand was insufficient tended to reduce the value of the currency concerned; this fuelled inflation and made it even more difficult to borrow the money needed to finance the deficits. The financial markets were advised by clever young men who were particularly susceptible to changes in academic fashion – 'teenage scribblers', as Nigel Lawson was to call them after he had ceased to be one himself. These advisers were mainly converts to the monetarist theories popularised by Milton Friedman; they began worrying about the monetary statistics, believing that inflation depended wholly on the money supply.

I have never met a private or central banker who believed the monetarist mumbo-jumbo. But no banker could afford to ignore monetarism as long as the markets took it seriously. So a conflict developed in Whitehall between unreconstructed Keynesians and unbelieving monetarists ... The theoretical conflict existed even inside the IMF itself.

Denis Healey, *The Time of my Life*, London, 1989, pp. 432–4.

## 3.10 The deficit on manufactured trade

In 1983 Britain imported more manufactured goods than she exported, for the first time in more than two centuries. Poor export performance and rising import penetration had been occurring in most categories of industrial production since the mid–1960s.

*Manufactured goods – the balance of trade and output*

The UK's balance of trade in manufactures has historically been in surplus. Between 1963 and 1983 exports of manufactures exceeded imports by between £1.5 billion and £6 billion every year. But in 1983 the balance of trade in manufactures moved into deficit for the first time. The deterioration was sharp, falling from a surplus of £5.5 billion in 1980 to a deficit of nearly £4 billion in 1984 – a deficit which is equal to 8.25 per cent of manufactured exports and 1.2 per cent of GDP.

The fall into deficit came suddenly, but the deterioration of exports as a ratio of imports had in fact been taking place over a long period. As time passed the country had been exporting relatively less and importing relatively more ... [I]n 1963 exports of manufactured goods were 2.75 times as large as imports. By 1973, most of this surplus had been eliminated. Despite two periods of recovery since then, the decline continued until in 1983 imports exceeded exports for the first time ...

Because of relatively poor export performance and import penetration, manufacturing has suffered at a time when growth in the economy has also been low. The consequence ... has been a fall in manufacturing output of 14.5 per cent in just the two years 1980 and 1981. Indeed, manufacturing has still not yet recovered to its

1979 level. While GDP has risen over the period 1972–84 taken as a whole, manufacturing output as a percentage of GDP has declined – from 28 per cent of GDP in 1972 to 21 per cent in 1983 – and the trend appears still to be downward. It is clear that manufacturing industry has been declining for the last decade in both absolute and relative terms.

House of Lords, *Report from the Select Committee on Overseas Trade*, London, 1985.

## 3.11 In and out of the Exchange Rate Mechanism

In October 1990 sterling joined the Exchange Rate Mechanism of the European Monetary System. In September 1992 sterling left after sustained market pressure against the ERM exchange rate. This article explains why the brief experiment was undertaken.

Shortly after the British government withdrew the pound from Europe's exchange-rate mechanism on 16 September, Norman Lamont, the Chancellor of the Exchequer, heaped blame on Germany and said that economic policy would henceforth serve British, not European, interests. John Major, the Prime Minister, agreed, saying Britain would not rejoin the ERM of the European monetary system until its 'fault lines' were repaired. Concluding that sterling would not rejoin quickly, the markets bet on lower British interest rates ...

A kindly view of all this is that the government has been shaken out of its wits. More worrying is the possibility that the government knows what it is doing – and is abandoning not merely the means but the aims of its previous policy.

*From force majeure to force Major*

To restore sense to British policy it is necessary to understand what went wrong. Mr Lamont was correct to blame Germany's Bundesbank for its part in the crisis of 16 September; it was inexcusable for the central bank that anchored the system to talk down a currency under pressure. But it was absurd of Mr Lamont to announce that his policy would henceforth be attuned to British interests as though, hitherto, it had not been.

If the Chancellor believed, even before the recent drama, that membership of the ERM failed to solve British interests, he should indeed resign for having assented to it. And if Mr Major and his Chancellor think, as they appear to, that the principal 'fault line' in the ERM was Germany's reluctance to alter its policies to help other ERM countries in distress, they have failed to make even a casual study of how the ERM has worked. For years the system's ability to exert discipline on governments unable to curb inflation for themselves rested precisely in the Bundesbank's narrow-minded concern with its own economy. The 'fault line' was, in fact, the whole point.

Successive British governments, of every political stripe, have shown themselves incapable of controlling inflation; British firms, workers and popular opinion have long been addicted to the same soft option. Within the ERM, countries also hooked have beaten the habit. That was why joining the system was in Britain's interests, and why – if it survives as an anti-inflationary force – sterling should go back in. The extraordinary stresses on the system of late, due to German unification, have not discredited the goals of low inflation and exchange rate stability. If the system endures with its necessary 'fault lines' intact, the question for Britain should not be whether to rejoin, but when, and what to do until then.

Sadly it would be folly to put the pound back into the ERM soon ... Sterling cannot safely rejoin the ERM until its decline is stopped and German interest rates have fallen by at least two or three percentage points from their present level.

Until then, the government must do whatever it can to dampen the self-fulfilling expectations of higher inflation that are already forming ... As the Chancellor has said, the government must monitor a range of indicators – broad and narrow money, asset prices (notably house prices), the exchange rate – and raise interest rates if they flash red. A bit vague? Why yes. A clear rule for economic policy has been abandoned: discretion must take its place. Those celebrating the economy's 'escape' from the ERM presumably feel that Mr Lamont is a man who can be trusted.

Discretion, however, has made a bad start. This week's cut in interest rates was ill-advised. From its floor in the ERM, sterling has already depreciated by 8 per cent; from its central rate, the fall is 14 per cent.[18] This represents, by itself, a considerable easing of policy; even if it goes no further, Britain's inflation rate in 1993 might be two or more percentage points higher than it would otherwise have been. Granted, the economy is weak and the indebtedness of consumers has made dear money a risky policy. These are good arguments against higher rates. But to cut rates, hinting at more to come, with sterling in mid-collapse and an easing of policy already working through, was reckless.

Which is why discretion needs to be placed in safer hands than the Treasury's. Finance Ministers are prone to make a hash of monetary policy because at times in every economic cycle there are more votes for inflation than for disinflation – even though inflation today makes the task of disinflation tomorrow (i.e. after the next election) all the more painful. Without delay, the government should announce that it will make an independent central Bank of England solely responsible for decisions on interest rates.

*The Economist*, 26 September 1992.

# 4
# The Labour Market

There have been three major developments in the labour market since 1945. The first has seen the replacement of 'full employment' during the 1970s by mass unemployment and much greater cyclical instability. Secondly, the labour force has changed from one dominated by males, working full-time and divided almost evenly between industry and services to the present position where women comprise almost half the total work force, where part-timers form a large and rapidly growing proportion of the labour force and where service sector work predominates. Finally, there have been significant changes over time in the behaviour of money wages.

## 4.1 The politics and ethics of full employment

> Full employment emerged during wartime as an overriding goal for post-war policy. In some respects this new, high priority reflected naked political realities, with the rise in status of both the industrial and political wings of organised labour. But there were also higher motives – a belief that in a civilised society the state should take the responsibility of organising the economic machine to produce employment for all its citizens.

Full employment is something more than one among many peace aims, just as unemployment is fundamental among contemporary social evils and the most corrosive of them. Work recognised by both the individual himself and by the community as possessing value is a necessary condition of the integrity and dignity of the human personality. This truth has branded itself on the consciousness of a generation which has knowingly maintained a large army of potential workers in idleness and assumed that its essential duty to them had been discharged if it saved them from sheer hunger. To provide useful work in satisfying conditions for the mass of the people is for the future an obligation as imperative as the obligation to provide them with food and shelter. It is also a primary political necessity. Full employment is a major premiss of far more than the Beveridge report. A policy of full employment, and confidence that the government have the will and the power to make it effective, are conditions without which the most carefully laid plans for orderly demobilisation after the war will go astray. The prospect of full employment is the one consideration which will allow both labour and capital to depart from the restrictive policies of the past and give to the industrial system that mobility of labour and flexibility of investment which it so urgently requires. Full employment is the key to economic policy, national and international, after the war.

*The Times*, 9 April 1943.

## 4.2 The danger of inflation

It did not take long for the first post-war government to accuse the labour movement of failing in its responsibilities for effective employment policy. This is the first draft of a white paper on the responsibilities of both sides of industry under a full employment policy. The TUC managed to tone down the criticisms of workpeople in the final published version.

Since 1941, our internal prices over a large part of ordinary consumers' expenditure have been kept steady by government action, partly through price controls and partly by government subsidies. The cost-of-living-index, which in December 1941 was 30 per cent above September 1939, is still only about 31 per cent above it today.[1] This result has only been achieved at heavy cost to the Exchequer ...

While the prices of essentials were kept steady by these means, wage adjustments took place during the war at almost regular intervals. During each of the years ended June 1942, 1943, 1944 and 1945, wage rates rose by 6 or 7 per cent of the pre-war level. These adjustments were generally of a short-term character, since it was impossible to forecast the trend of events over a long period ahead. When the war ended, a new situation developed. It was possible, over a wide field of industry, to make provision for post-war settlements. As a result, during the twelve months ending July 1946, wage rates rose by thirteen points, making a total increase of 64 per cent since September 1939. The table illustrates the broad relations between earnings, wage rates and the cost-of-living-index since 1939.

| *Avg. weekly earnings* | | *Basic wage rates* | *Cost-of-living index* |
|---|---|---|---|
| 100 (1938) | September 1939 | 100 | 100 |
| 130 | Mid–1940 | 112 | 121 |
| 160 | Mid–1942 | 131 | 129 |
| 182 | Mid–1944 | 143 | 130 |
| 189 | Mid–1946 | 161 | 132 |
| – | November 1946 | 164 | 131 |

The direct gains have been considerable. The thirteen points increase in wage rates since July 1945, reckoned in terms of the 1945 wage bill, is roughly equivalent to £250 million. The total increase of sixty-four points since the beginning of the war, reckoned in terms of the 1939 wage bill, is roughly equivalent to £1,200 million a year. Moreover, over a large field of industry, the trade unions have gained for their members not only higher wages and earnings but many improvements in conditions, such as holidays with pay and a guaranteed week. The government and the country desire that these gains should be consolidated and become a permanent advance in real wages. But this desire will be frustrated if the only effect is to produce increases in costs and prices. How then is the desire to be achieved?

*Production*

The answer first and last is by increasing production. The gains in wage rates which have been achieved have not yet been matched by an equivalent increase in output. They do represent an increase in purchasing power because the increase has been kept down by the subsidies, so that the increase of wage rates has greatly outstripped the cost-of-living index. But to achieve a genuine balance between the volume of purchasing power and the supply of goods available there must be a big increase in production ...

How is this increase of production to be obtained? By ensuring that those industries which provide essential supplies are fully manned up; by maintaining full employment so that we can make use of all the manpower we can muster; and by raising the level of output per head while costs and prices are held steady.

*Essential supplies*

We must concentrate first on increasing production in those home industries which supply the vital materials required for the necessities of life. This is not only essential if we are to achieve the standard of life which full employment should ensure, but it is even more urgent in the short run to break the shortages of basic materials which are holding up the whole process of reconversion of civilian life and industry. Many of the industries responsible for producing these materials are seriously short of workers, and the very fact that full employment now exists has created great difficulties in the way of bringing them up to strength. They are largely industries which have suffered from depression in the past or from concentration[2] during the war. If other industries compete too strongly with them for labour, not only will they be unable to satisfy the demands of the people of this country for a better standard of consumption, but they will be unable to produce the goods which are vital to all other production. The existence of these shortages is a standing threat to the employment of workers in other industries and services, who may find themselves without the fuel or raw materials on which their jobs depend. It is therefore a matter of overriding concern to all employers and workers that these essential industries should be brought up to the necessary strength without delay.

*Full employment*

At the present time there is some local unemployment … but the government is taking energetic measures to remedy this … If patches of unemployment occur in the immediate future because of shortages of supplies, they will be temporary and they will be righted as soon as the shortages can be made good … this means that the old fear of prolonged bad trade and unemployment should be a thing of the past. Instead, we want a new determination to achieve higher standards and increased output. Bad trade and unemployment in the inter-war years led to cutting of wages and prices and losses to all concerned. The problem today is to increase production to fill the gap between the quantity of goods on the market and the wage increases which have already been obtained. We must remove the idea of spinning out production in order to avoid unemployment, or of restricting output in order to safeguard earnings. On the contrary, industry must be ready to adopt every possible means of increasing production, secure in the knowledge that this does not carry with it any threat to employment. Indeed, without high production full employment itself is endangered.

'Joint Consultative Committee: Statement on the economic considerations affecting the relations between employers and workers', Public Record Office, LAB 10/655, no date.

## 4.3 Unions and productivity

As the previous extract indicates, the trade unions were under great pressure to encourage workers to accept changes which would accelerate productivity growth. The TUC found itself in a similar position in both the 1950s and the 1960s. The following is the TUC response to pressure for faster diffusion of techniques of 'automation' in the mid–1950s.

*Problems for trade unions*

Besides having human, social and economic implications, automation has implications also for trade unions – although not necessarily substantially different in kind from those caused by everyday productivity-increasing industrial developments. The scale and speed of application of automation may, of course, sharpen some of the problems – particularly those related to labour displacement, changes in skill requirements and trade union organising. It is probable that craft unions organising workpeople on maintenance and the unions catering for technical personnel will gain at the expense of unions having as members semi-skilled operatives engaged in direct production ...

Another feature of large-scale automation is that with new jobs, new fatigues[3] and new responsibilities, it cannot have other than a heavy impact on wages and working conditions, not only in the industries concerned but, because of national and industry-wide negotiations, in other industries also. Unions will undoubtedly seek to spread any advantages and benefits secured in automation industries throughout industry generally. A negotiating problem for trade unions is that the present by and large piecemeal introduction of automatic processes is being fitted into existing wage structures which do not necessarily reflect automation's 'ability to pay' or provide improved conditions of work – since labour costs will form only a small percentage of total production costs.

The major job of the trade unions will be to keep automation within the field of industrial relations; countering assumptions that working conditions, earning opportunities, pace of working and other matters affecting workpeople can or should be arbitrarily fixed by machines or technicians – that there is no opportunity for joint negotiations and the expression of trade union points of view on questions connected with industrial efficiency and development. Automation can make a substantial contribution to social well-being, but there is no automatic transfer system to ensure this. The trade unions will see as one of their main duties the performing of this function.

TUC, 'Automation', Scientific Advisory Committee Paper 1/1, 31 January 1955, held at Modern Records Centre, University of Warwick, MSS 292/571.81/5A.

## 4.4 Tripartite policy-making

TUC leaders and prominent industrialists were routinely consulted about economic policy in the years before 1979. Union leaders were frequently under pressure to hold back the pace of wage increases, as in this instance – the minutes of a crisis meeting at Chequers in August 1955. The impression that TUC leaders sympathised with government wishes to control wage increases is widespread in the documents in the 1950s.

*The Chancellor of the Exchequer*[4] recalled how the situation had developed in recent years. We had had a great surge of expansion after the period of wartime and post-war restrictions. At the same time full employment had been maintained. This was a common objective of both parties. He himself, when Parliamentary Secretary at the Ministry of Labour in the 1930s had seen the effects of unemployment at first hand. The situation had been kept in hand until developments at the beginning of the year made it necessary to try to restrict credit expansion ... There was not a crisis but the present position gave cause for anxiety. Our foreign exchange position was not satisfactory. In relation to the dollar area we were holding our own but there was still uncertainty in Europe. At home local authorities would also have to bear their share of the reduction of investment. All unnecessary work, whether public or private, needed to be held back.

*Sir Graham Hayman*[5] said that action by the government to restrict its own expenditure and investment would have a very salutary effect on opinion. Secondly, while he understood the general arguments in favour of keeping down prices, it was difficult to persuade individual industrialists to reduce prices at a time when internal demand was so buoyant and when they were faced both with the financing of development and with increasing wage claims.

*Mr Geddes*[6] said that he had to make a speech and to guide the Trades Union Congress. He would doubtless be rather critical of the government but he wanted to do what was right in the interests of the unions and the country as a whole. He wanted to know whether or not there really was a crisis. In the present conditions it was difficult to persuade the workers that they ought to hold back on wage claims. Industry was making profits and prices were rising. Moreover was it true that our exports were really in danger? Unless it were known that the situation was serious, any plea for restraint which he might intend to make would certainly not be listened to.

*Mr Heywood*[7] emphasised the difficulties of getting the issues understood by the workers, particularly those not connected with the export industries, in present conditions. Unless there was some stability in prices, there was no hope of wage restraint.

*Sir Vincent Tewson*[8] said that the TUC had itself given repeated warnings and had indeed taken a rather critical view of government economic policy in budgets in recent years. They had a difficult line to hold.

'Summary of a meeting held at Chequers on Monday, 29 August 1955' Public Record Office T 234/17.

## 4.5 Skill shortages

One of the characteristics of the period of full employment was the tendency of companies to 'hoard' labour, particularly skilled workers, so that they might respond quickly to any increase in demand for their products. However, companies unable to pass on the costs of carrying under-utilised and expensive workers found themselves competing for very scarce craftsmen during periods of economic expansion, with the result that wages began to rise rapidly. Any attempt to raise the growth rate had to find an answer to 'skill shortages'.

*The shortages*

Shortages of craftsmen have prevailed in this country for most of the post-war period. The shortages are not at present acute except in certain trades but they can be expected to reappear in conditions of faster economic growth because the higher level of demand and more rapid technological advance will increase the demand for skilled manpower. The welcome increase in the apprenticeship intake since 1958, due largely to the efforts of the Ministry of Labour, the Industrial Training Council and both sides of industry to persuade employers to expand training during the period of the 'school leaving bulge',[9] will increase the flow of skilled craftsmen within the period but ... this does not seem likely to be sufficient to meet to meet the shortages. It is very necessary for future growth that apprenticeship training should continue to increase during the next five years but this will make little direct contribution to the skilled labour force during the period. An expansion of adult training facilities will therefore be required to meet the demand for various types and degrees of skill.

*Adult training*

Most of the training and retraining of adults is done within industry and there needs to be a further expansion of this training during the next five years, particularly in the less prosperous regions, to meet the requirements of incoming firms[10] ... Comparatively few opportunities for retraining skilled workers who need to change their employer as well as their occupation are provided within industry. It seems therefore that it will be necessary for the Ministry of Labour to play a bigger role in providing adult training facilities for redundant workers or other workers who want to change their jobs.

National Economic Development Council, *Conditions Favourable to Faster Growth*, London, 1963, p. 7.

## 4.6 Industrial relations in the 1960s – the Donovan analysis

The Wilson government established a Royal Commission under Lord Donovan in April 1965 to inquire into the effects on economic growth of the British system of industrial relations. The quoted extract is taken from the report's conclusions.

Britain has two systems of industrial relations. One is the formal system embodied in the official institutions. The other is the informal system created by the actual behaviour of trade unions and employers' associations, of managers, shop stewards and workers.

The keystone of the formal system is the industry-wide collective agreement, in which are supposed to be settled pay, hours of work and other conditions of employment appropriate to regulation by agreement.

The informal system is often at odds with the formal system. Actual earnings have moved far apart from the rates laid down in industry-wide agreements; the three main elements in the 'gap' are piecework or incentive earnings, company or factory additions to basic rates, and overtime earnings. These are all governed by decisions within the factory ... At the same time, disputes procedures laid down in industry-wide agreements have been subjected to strain by the transfer of authority to the factory and the workshop.

The bargaining which takes place within factories is largely outside the control of employers' associations and trade unions. It usually takes place piecemeal and results in competitive sectional wage adjustments and chaotic pay structures. Unwritten understandings and 'custom and practice' predominate.

These developments help to explain why resort to unofficial and unconstitutional strikes and other forms of workshop pressure has been increasing.

This decentralisation of collective bargaining has taken place under the pressure of full employment, which in Britain has had special consequences because of the way our industrial organisations have reacted to it.

The authority of employers' organisations has declined. At one time they were innovators, but from 1914 until very recently nearly every important innovation in industrial relations which was not the work of the unions came from the government or from individual companies.

Despite this decline, however, most individual companies do not have comprehensive and well-ordered agreements for regulating terms and conditions over and above industry-wide minima. There has been a growth in the importance of personnel specialists, but many companies have no effective personnel policy to control methods of negotiation and pay structure and perhaps no conception of one.

Shop stewards are to be found in most factories where unions are strong. The basis of the shop steward's power is the work group. Full employment would in any case have increased the influence of work groups but the way managements have chosen to act has also augmented it.

Trade unions have, like employers' organisations and managers, helped to sustain the facade of industry-wide bargaining, but cannot bear primary responsibility for the decline in its effectiveness. However, certain features of trade union structure and government have helped to inflate the power of work groups and shop stewards. One is the existence of multi-unionism in most British industries and factories.

The government's influence has generally been used to support the arrangements which have developed in private industry, and statutory wage fixation and systems of wage settlement in the public services for the most part yield results not very dissimilar from those achieved by collective bargaining elsewhere.

Many of those who conduct industrial relations in Britain are content with things as they are, because the arrangements are comfortable and flexible and provide a very high degree of self-government. Existing arrangements can be condemned only because these important benefits are outweighed by the disadvantages: the tendency of extreme decentralisation and self-government to degenerate into indecision and anarchy; the propensity to breed inefficiency; and the reluctance to change. All these characteristics become more damaging as they develop, as the rate of technical progress increases and the need for economic growth becomes more urgent.

*Royal Commission on Trade Unions and Employers' Organisations, 1965–1968: Report*, London, 1968 (Cmnd 3623), pp. 261–2.

## 4.7 Women in employment

Although the vocabulary of many of the previous extracts shows that commentators conceived of a labour force which was predominantly male, in reality circumstances were changing, with women comprising a growing proportion of the total work force and, among them, a large share of part-time workers.

A major factor in the expansion of the labour force in recent years has been the increasing number of women taking paid employment. The increase has been greatest in the numbers and proportion of married women at work. However, there are wide differences between industries in the numbers and proportion of women employees but there is very little variation between different parts of the country in the extent of women's employment.

*Change over fifty years*

The most striking difference in the economic activity rates of single women between 1921 and 1971 is not at the beginning of normal working life, but in the later age groups. The proportion of single women at work in their early twenties was already eight out of ten in 1921. (The actual percentage was a little higher in 1971.) Whereas in 1921, however, the older they were the less likely they were to be working, in 1971 the proportion of single women in the work force, full-time or part-time, actually went up in the later twenties (on completion of education and training) and thereafter maintained a relatively high level right into the middle fifties. Whereas fifty years ago only half of all single women of that age were economically active, more than three-quarters of them were in 1971.

Greater changes have occurred in the extent to which married women are in paid employment ... [I]n 1921 a small minority of young married women in their early twenties (just over one in ten) were at work, whereas nearly half were in 1971. Moreover the 1971 figures show a continuous increase in the economic activity of married women between the ages of thirty and fifty. From the mid-fifties the proportion of women, whether married or single, going out to work declines – just as does the proportion of men – and it drops off quite rapidly for those who have reached sixty, which is the minimum age for national insurance retirement pension for women – just as the men's rates show a sharp fall after sixty-five, their minimum pension age ...

*Contributory factors*

Commenting on the trend in economic activity rates for women, the Department of Employment point out that the causes of these developments are complex and not all can be quantified. In the past it was usual for a woman to leave work when she married. Now it is more usual for her to stay at work until the first child is due. With smaller families and less time between children the period of time while a woman has children under school age is considerably reduced, and her total absence from the work force for bringing up her family is much shorter than in previous generations. It is also now more socially acceptable for a woman with dependent children to be in employment.

In addition to this, mass production and advances in technology have combined to produce many labour saving devices, convenience foods, cleaning materials, easy-care fabrics and so on, which reduce the amount of time necessary to do domestic chores. The service industries have also developed to cater increasingly for the needs of the working woman.

*Industrial distribution*

The total number of women employees in Great Britain recorded in the Department of Employment census of employment at June 1973 was 8.7 million, compared with 13.5 million men.

The significance of part-time work[11] in women's employment is shown by the fact that over 3 million out of the 8.7 million women – rather more than one in three – were part-time workers, compared with about one in twenty of the men ... [I]n general the industry groups which employ most women are also those where there are most women working part-time.

Part-time employment is less common in manufacturing than in other industries but ... there has been a marked expansion of part-time work in manufacturing in the last twenty years.

The largest number of women, and the most in proportion to total employees, were found ... in the service industry groups (which are also the largest employers of men). In four service industry groups women outnumbered men. These were the professional and scientific services, which include teachers, nursing and social work; the 'miscellaneous' group, which includes workers in hotels, restaurants and pubs, laundries and hairdressing, and which had the highest proportion of part-time workers in the whole census; the distributive trades; and insurance, banking and similar services. In only one of the manufacturing industry groups, clothing and footwear, was there a preponderance of women over men employees.

*Economic Progress Report*, 56, November 1974.

## 4.8 The shortage of engineers

The labour market implications of the microelectronic revolution placed enormous strain and emphasis on the supply of technologists, particularly of engineers. Another Royal Commission (under Sir Monty Finniston) was appointed to examine the situation.

The industrial society of the future has to adapt not just to the consequences of past changes but also to the enhanced rate of change which new technology and its adoption throughout the world are creating and will continue to create as long as can be foreseen; microprocessors are just one example of future shock. In the introduction and management of these changes the main thrust lies in the area of engineering. Without highly educated and trained engineers, continually updating their skills and given authority and influence in concert with other industrially biased disciplines to implement the products of those skills, there can be no confident prospect of stemming the decline of the British economy relative to its international competitors.

In our deliberations we have from the start been concerned with the 'wider issue' of the future economic health of this country. We have argued that this economic future, and hence the welfare and standard of living of this nation, depends upon the degree of its success in achieving growth in the output of its manufacturing industries, in terms of marketable products and of systems of services based on their use and of the efficiency with which these are provided to customers throughout the world. The commissioning of these tasks depends upon a variety of contributions, some direct and some indirect, and also upon the extent to which the people concerned with the separate contributions perceive common aims and how well they relate together in progressing the national interest in their activities.

Within companies it requires those determining the strategy and direction of manufacturing enterprises to recognise the need to relate technical capability to market needs; to ensure that they employ sufficient people with the necessary expertise; and to use, develop and organise the contributions of those people to fullest effect. Among engineers it demands a wide perception of their role within the enterprise and in particular the willingness and capability to relate their technical knowledge to its commercial objectives and the demands of its customers. Within the government and other sectors determining the commitment and distribution of resources within the economy – be they financial or human – it requires a recognition of shared direct interest in the success of companies achieving their objectives and wholehearted support for their endeavours to do so; in the education sector it requires astute perception of the kinds of skills and understanding demanded of those who will lead and carry through engineering-based changes in industry and elsewhere and provision to cater for those demands; and in all other bodies and institutions concerned with the industry and/or engineers it demands concomitant positive support through their respective activities ...

Against this background of change the skills of the present generation of engineers must be deployed to greater effect than hitherto, not just at technical operating levels, but in the decision-making processes of companies and industrial sectors, and they must be given the authority and encouragement to influence and implement policies at that level as well as at the higher levels of community and nation. In addition it is necessary to attract, recruit, educate and train sufficient new engineers. This requires changes in attitudes and practices throughout society: in schools, universities and polytechnics, in institutions (technical, professional or political), in the machinery of national and local government and its agencies; but above all by industry in its deployment and development of engineering skills and engineers.

*Engineering our Future: Report of the Committee of Inquiry into the Engineering Profession* (the Finniston report), London, 1980 (Cmnd 7794), pp. 158–60.

## 4.9 The causes of mass unemployment in the 1980s

More than forty years after the famous *Employment Policy* white paper of 1944, unemployment again disfigured British economic and social life. A sharp recovery from the deep slump of 1979–82 initially failed to make any real impact on mass unemployment. The government issued a new white paper, this time placing the onus for employment creation on the private rather than the public sector and on the individual rather than the state.

### Learning the lessons

#### *The basis for jobs*

Jobs come from customers and from nowhere else. That simple and enduring truth must underlie any useful discussion of employment. Jobs are created when businesses produce goods and services that people want at prices they can afford. When businesses succeed they create wealth and make jobs, not only for their own employees but also for other people whose goods and services those employees buy and for the public services and welfare which their taxes fund. Public-service employment, however valuable, has to be paid for, and by one route or another the money can come in the end only from businesses. If the burden becomes too high, businesses shrink or fail, and jobs are lost with them.

Ours is an open trading economy, and with exports equivalent to nearly a third of our gross domestic product we depend heavily on overseas orders. This means competing with other countries in initiative, in quality and design, in marketing and service, and in prices and costs. If we do not give good value for money our products will not sell abroad, nor even at home. The consequences then fall not just on the trading sector of our economy but ultimately on everyone. We all depend directly or indirectly on one another. If a particular sector prospers, the gains feed right through in extra revenue to provide better public services and social benefits for all; if it fails, the taxes of the rest have to help bear the penalties. And the worst of the penalties is unemployment.

Unemployment rises when we move too slowly to meet new consumer needs, overseas competition and technological change, and when pay and prices – the link between supply and demand – adjust too slowly. There is no basic lack of demand; the reason why we cannot use our full labour force is that we have not adapted well enough, particularly in our jobs market, to be able to exploit it.

To put this right and create jobs the people of Britain have to:

- show enterprise and a willingness to take risks
- respond and adapt continually to new ideas and changing circumstances
- carry out the necessary research and development
- combine labour, materials and capital to produce efficiently and on time
- pay ourselves realistically
- market imaginatively
- communicate effectively
- serve customers well
- take a proper pride in craftsmanship
- welcome new technology

And we have to do this at least as well as it is done in other countries, if we want to match their standards of living. As the list shows, the task needs a concerted national effort. In the end jobs depend on the enterprise, attitude and skill of everyone involved in industry and commerce.

*Past failures*

For most of the time since 1950 living standards have been rising throughout the Western world. But they have generally risen less in Britain than elsewhere; and the reason is that our economy has been less efficient.

- Between 1960 and 1982, average productivity in manufacturing industry grew by over 500 per cent in Japan, over 120 per cent in the Federal Republic of Germany and under 80 per cent in the UK. Yet we tried to pay ourselves as though we were achieving top international standards ... In Japan the pay increase was roughly double the productivity increase; in the Federal Republic of Germany three times; in the USA four times; and in the UK, over ten times.

• Both managers and workers too often failed to put the customer first. Management often failed its work force, for lack of resolve and professionalism: and did not react to the realities of competition. Despite our impressive record in research and invention, many of our industries fell behind international standards of product, design, price, delivery, service and investment ...

• Many workers, especially those in powerful unions, felt they could escape the discomfort of new ways of working and hold economic reality at bay, often by strikes and the threat of them; some behaved as if their jobs would always be there, no matter what they or anyone else did. Companies were burdened by overmanning and outdated methods.

• Governments, albeit with the best of intentions, handicapped business with too much regulation and intervention, and too little stability of policy. Business decision-making was distorted by misplaced incentives, and by excessive and ill-directed taxation.

• The entrepreneur, whose initiative and risk-taking link customers to jobs and are the key to wealth creation for all, was undervalued, neglected and sometimes actively discouraged ...

Many of our industries – shipbuilding, motor cycles, cars – paid a high price for shortcomings like these. In the 1970s the effects became increasingly widespread. The oil price rises of 1973 and 1979 set off a recession which hit all industrialised countries: but it hit us harder than most, because we were more vulnerable and less adaptable. Inflation moreover got out of control, and that made things worse.

Against this background, and despite ever-growing public spending, the jobless numbers mounted. They doubled between 1971 and 1977 and doubled again by 1982 – in large measure as the disguised unemployment of earlier years, with overmanning rife, was forced into the open. The rise has been stemmed but not entirely halted. If we are to reverse it, we need to understand first the facts of our employment situation and then what we all need to do about it.

*Employment: The Challenge for the Nation*, London, 1985 (Cmnd 9474), pp. 3–5.

## 4.10 Not much to show for the labour market legislation of the 1980s

Union restrictions were identified as a significant cause of unemployment and slow growth by Thatcher governments. In the mid–1990s, after fifteen years of progressive erosion of trade union power, the benefits of anti-union legislation seem unclear.

In 1979, the trade union movement stood condemned as the main agent of Britain's economic decline, guilty of fostering inefficient work practices and inflationary pay settlements. Fifteen years later ... the movement is a shadow of its former self. But where is the evidence that the economy has benefited as a result?

The humbling of the unions has been more dramatic than even the most hardened free-marketeer could have wished. Membership has dropped from nearly 13.3 million in 1979 to around 7.2 million in 1994. This has cut the proportion of the work force with union membership from more than a half to barely a third. Collective bargaining over pay and conditions now takes place in only a minority of workplaces, compared to nearly three-quarters in the mid–1970s.

Several factors explain this decline. Some economists blame it entirely on higher unemployment. Rising joblessness has certainly done the unions no favours, but remember that their membership continued to drop even when unemployment was falling fast.

The changing composition of the work force may be more important. Unions have never been very good at recruiting women, part-timers, non-manual workers and people in service industries. All these groups have been growing at the expense of the unions' traditionally male and blue-collar constituency ...

But the government's step-by-step legislative attack on the unions is surely the most important cause of their emasculation. Statutory procedures for union recognition have been abolished, picketing limited, the closed shop outlawed, legal immunities weakened and pre-strike ballots enforced. It is hardly surprising that strike activity has fallen to record lows ...

The combination of adverse legislation and an unfavourable economic tide has tipped the balance of power away from the unions and towards management. As a result, unions have found it increasingly difficult to deliver the goods. In 1984, semi-skilled employees in a unionised workplace earned 8 per cent more than their non-unionised counterparts. By 1990, this mark-up had dropped to 6 per cent and has presumably shrunk even further since then ...

But the evidence that the decline of the unions has boosted employment and other measures of economic performance is much less clear-cut. Professors David Blanchflower and Richard Freeman have ... concluded that the reforms had made employment and wage levels a little more flexible at company level, but had failed to make wages more responsive to changing unemployment in the economy as a whole ... But the attack on the unions may have been the right policy at the wrong time. Blanchflower and Freeman argue that the Thatcher reforms might have done wonders when the economy was running at near full employment in the 1950s and 1960s, but not when unemployment became so high.

High unemployment results in rising long-term unemployment.[12] The long-term jobless cannot compete for existing workers' jobs because they become demotivated and unattractive to employers.[13] This means that there is less pressure on 'insiders' with jobs to moderate their wage claims. This could explain why the wages of those in work remain as high as they do ...

The assault on the unions certainly does not appear to have yielded the scale of economic benefits that might have been expected fifteen years ago. We cannot be sure, because it is impossible to disentangle the impact of the Thatcher reforms from the catastrophic mismanagement of macroeconomic policy that has accompanied them. But as the recovery gains in strength, it would be dangerous to act as though the crusade against the unions had really delivered the economic miracle claimed for it.

Robert Chote, 'Not much to show for smashing the unions', *Independent on Sunday*, 11 September 1994.

# 5

# Assessments of the Causes of Relative Decline

The range of explanations for Britain's relative economic decline is vast. This chapter illustrates three broad types of interpretation: those from within what might be called the 'post-war consensus'; those which locate the blame in uniquely British institutions, often with roots deep in Britain's past; and those which portray the 'post-war consensus' as an important part of the problem.

## 5.1 Within the consensus, 1: inadequate statistics and economics

> In the confident days of the mid–1950s it was becoming clear that the British economy was performing less well than expected, but the problems appeared to be relatively superficial – probably the result of poorly timed policy interventions which were in turn caused by the inadequacies of official statistics and the imperfections of economic knowledge.

From the financial prospects for the Exchequer during the coming year, following the normal course of these speeches, I now turn to the economic prospects. Here, alas, there is no true science which can give us certainty in this uncertain field. Some people feel that what passes for such is more like astrology than astronomy. Lyndoe or Old Moore may turn out just as reliable as Professor What's-his-name or Dr So-and-so. I do not share this extreme view. Nevertheless, I think we should all agree that if there is such a science, it is not an exact one. There are too many unknowns and too many variables. Then I am told that some of our statistics are too late to be as useful as they ought to be. We are always, as it were, looking up a train in last year's Bradshaw.[1]

Some of my friends on both sides of the House feel this strongly ... these friends of mine think that some means ought to be found to get us earlier information of what will happen and to devise more precise and perfect weapons for dealing with trouble both before and when it comes ... I am still conscious of a certain gap in our defences in this matter and the need to strengthen our technical and administrative armoury. We must continually improve our statistics, in form and timing. We shall, of course, have to make further calls on the co-operation of industry. I am sure that this will be readily given. More complete and more up-to-date information will not only help in the proper ordering of the national economy, but will help industries themselves by enabling them to foresee more accurately the conditions in which they have to operate.

Harold Macmillan, Budget speech, *House of Commons Debates*, 17 April 1956, cols. 865–7.

## 5.2 Within the consensus, 2: a failure of tripartite structures

By the early 1960s the machinery of economic policy-making and the range of government statistics were much broader than in the 1950s but faster growth was as elusive as ever. The 'incorporation' of union leaders into policy-making placed them in a difficult political position, which they were happiest to avoid. Conservative Ministers blamed the failure of the 1960s 'dash for growth' on the unions and began to revert to their traditional hostility towards trade unionism.

The real problem of the domestic economy was how to achieve a steady and adequate rate of growth without inflation. This problem has baffled successive Chancellors in the past, as it has done ever since. We had done a lot of work on establishing the National Economic Development Council (NEDC) and we had begun the establishment of the National Incomes Commission (NIC). The idea behind these institutions was that government, management and the unions all had a part to play in establishing steady economic growth; they were interdependent and without co-operation between them the nation could not prosper. The government's basic responsibility was to find a policy for demand management which would ensure the full use of resources without generating fresh domestic inflation and without diverting resources from exports and thus undermining the balance of payments. We agreed at NEDC on a target growth rate of 4 per cent, which we thought could be sustained, being based on a combination of a 3.2 per cent rate of productivity growth, which historical data led us to think was practicable, as indeed it was; and a 0.8 per cent growth of the available labour force. One of the major tasks of NEDC was to eliminate obstacles to such a rate of growth and our conclusions were published in an official paper ...

Our belief was that within NEDC we could get broad agreement on the general level of wage increases that could be absorbed by the economy without further inflation, and in this proposition we were not unsuccessful. But, of course, the problem as always was the special case ... we sought a system whereby exceptions could be identified, and the reasons why they could be treated as exceptions clearly defined. So we hoped they would be able to remain exceptions and would not, by exciting the emotions involved in comparability, accelerate the whole pace of wage advance. It was a good idea ... Short of statutory control of incomes no one has so far produced a better one. But I am afraid it was frustrated very largely by the Trade Unions ...

The second danger was the balance of payments. The British economy had always shown since the War a very high propensity to import manufactured goods and semi-manufactures, and we would feel the strain of this, for ... it is quite obvious that you bring in your raw materials and components and have to pay for them before you can get the expansion of exports from their use, which provides you with the revenue. But our calculation was that any strain on the balance of payments would be temporary and that we had adequate borrowing facilities to tide over any short-term difficulties ... So we went for expansion, quite deliberately, with our eyes open, recognising the dangers. The prize to be obtained, the prospect of expansion without inflation, the end of stop-go and a break-out from the constrictions of the past, was a glittering one.

Reginald Maudling, *Memoirs*, London, 1978, pp. 111, 114–16.

## 5.3 Within the consensus, 3: industrial modernisation

The belated shift of the Conservatives to planning and other 'supply-side' measures in the early 1960s was skilfully exploited by Labour politicians, who argued that they had long been ideologically and politically committed to the interventionist policies required to 'modernise' the British economy. It was now agreed that fundamental changes were required in industry and that the state had an important role in modernisation.

Our weakness lies in the fact that in every crisis of the past few years we heaved a sigh of relief once the run on sterling had been dealt with by borrowing and perhaps interest rate policy, and failed to realise that this was the time to strengthen the economy which would inevitably stop the *next* period of expansion from ending in crisis ...

The one lesson of the past few years is that you don't make sterling strong by making the economy weak. We condemned attempts to solve our export-import problem by holding our production below the level of our industrial capacity. The key to a strong pound lies not in Britain's finances but in the nation's industry. Finance must be the index, not the determinant, of economic strength ...

The prime need of industry is for modernisation. We are being left behind each year by the USA, by Germany, by the USSR, even by France, in the pace of modernisation, particularly with automotive equipment. We are becoming desperately vulnerable. I suggest, therefore, that just as we once gave special tax encouragement to fuel-saving equipment we should give a decisive investment allowance on a speedy write-off, in respect of all expenditure, particularly named types of automotive equipment – at any rate in manufacturing industry ...

I would particularly stress the need to develop import-saving industries. This should be tackled with at least as much urgency as the exports drive ... The safest way to expand production without fear of an overseas trade crisis is to ensure that those products which swell our import bill at times of expansion are, as far as is technically possible, produced in this country. I am appalled at the big increase in machinery and semi-finished manufactures that have come into this country in the past few years. I cannot believe that British industry, with appropriate stimulus and help, cannot produce a lot more of these things on a competitive basis. I am not thinking in protectionist terms. I am thinking in terms of help with financing the necessary expansion ...

The other instrument we shall use is the creation of new publicly owned industries based on science. At Scarborough, I referred to the vast and costly research and development contracts which the government had placed in the past few years for missiles and military aircraft, in many cases hundreds of millions of pounds spent on weapons which did not get off the drawing board. What we want to see is research and development contracts aimed at giving us a new breakthrough in civil industry ...

What we now propose is that this sponsored research, to be carried out by government research institutions, private industry, and CATs[2] and technological departments of universities, should be sharply stepped up. This is why we have proposed in the House of Commons the creation of a Ministry of Technology to expand civil research and make it more purposive.

But we have asserted that where new industries develop, as a result of community-sponsored research, the community should have an appropriate share of the profits and the control. In some cases, this would mean state-owned industries – and because they were state-owned, we should be able to locate them in areas where work is needed, without all the paraphernalia of cajolery and bribery that is needed with some private enterprises. But others will be joint ventures between public and private ownership, and yet others will be based on licences granted on a royalty or profit-sharing basis.

Harold Wilson, 'Labour's economic policy', speech made at the Brangwyn Hall, Swansea, 25 January 1964, reprinted in *Labour's Plan outlined by Harold Wilson: Selected Speeches, 1964*, Harmondsworth, 1964, pp. 30–3.

## 5.4 Institutional constraints, 1: the establishment

Thomas Balogh was a powerful critic of the British civil service. His most sustained critique of the inability of the British administrative machine to make effective economic policy came in an essay, 'The apotheosis of the dilettante', published in a number of collections in the 1960s. Here he summarises his main conclusions.

*Unfit for the job*

The post-war record of British economic policy inevitably leads to the conclusion that a civil service reform as fundamental as that undertaken by Northcote and Trevelyan[3] is long overdue, even if Britain did not adopt a basically new policy ... Though the British civil service structure was evolved very late and received its final codification only after the first world war, it had been designed in 1854 for a negative, law-and-order state. For that purpose it was admirably conceived. The honesty and assiduity of the civil service is really beyond reproach, and constitutes the basis of its reputation. In this it contrasts very favourably indeed with conditions abroad.

But all reforms or changes undertaken since the turn of the century made it less rather than more responsive to the demands of the new positive welfare state. Almost all regular civil servants are recruited by competitive examination laying stress on intelligence. Expert knowledge, on the contrary, is not the basis of recruitment and is not encouraged by the system of training and promotion even as much as it was before 1914. Economists, for instance, are recruited into the civil service, as such, as either specialists or technicians only. Consequently they are under contract, not established and cannot in practice rise beyond a limited rank ... People who have a degree in economics can, of course, enter the general service through the competitive examination, but they are not necessarily assigned to departments dealing with economics, and even if they are, their having studied economics will only be coincidental.

When the NEDC was established and a search was made for men in the civil service trained in economics, they were found generally in non-economic jobs and the respective departments refused to release them on the plea that this would interfere with their career. Immediately after the war, economists entering as economic advisers could get established. This practice, however, has been discontinued. The movement of administrators not merely from one part of the department to another, but between departments, has encouraged an approach to problems incompatible with the requirements of positive policy-making. The expert is subordinated to the non-expert whose attitude necessarily is coloured by his lack of real understanding. The consequence is muddle.

*Safeguarding existing virtues*

It would be a pity if the constructive aspects of the present civil service organisation were to be destroyed. It should remain an independent corporate entity whose members enjoy security to safeguard independence of judgement. Its members should have a prospect of an honourable career. At the same time its present tight exclusiveness should be loosened (a one-sided loosening has already taken place inasmuch as a great number of high civil servants drift into directorships of important private companies). Expert knowledge, too, must be secured which is highly needed for the management of a modern welfare state, in bitter competition with other countries.

Thomas Balogh, *Planning for Progress: A Strategy for Labour*, Fabian Tract 346, London, 1963, pp. 30–2.

## 5.5 Institutional constraints, 2: the legacy of the past in industrial leadership

G. C. Allen was a leading applied economist and for many years the leading British authority on Japanese economic development and policy. He was one of the first to identify a 'British disease', which he located in the pattern of British industrialisation. Like Balogh, he criticised the 'cult of the amateur', but found the apotheosis of the dilettante in business leadership as much as in the bureaucracy.

We are thus led back to the proposition that industrial progress depends primarily on the quality of industrial leadership and we have to consider whether [after 1870] that quality had deteriorated since the great days [of the industrial revolution] and, if so, for what reasons ...

*Complacency by descendants of pioneers*

Complacency after a long period of success was perhaps to be expected ... The descendants of the pioneers are tempted to take things easy. The institutions created to serve one stage of development may prove to be intractable and frustrating at the next stage, but may survive nonetheless through the force of tradition and convention. This generalisation seems to describe what happened in Britain ...

*Disdain for trade*

Besides the general causes of decadence which ... are likely to afflict every civilisation in some stage of its development, there were present in Britain some special, and perhaps rather extraordinary, causes that converged to transform so many of the heirs of the great industrial innovators into complacent routineers ... In the seventeenth century, after the country was launched on its career as an international trader, those who made money as merchants naturally sought to elevate themselves into the class above them, the landed gentry. This was the path to social esteem and political and administrative power. They purchased country estates and married their daughters to the sons of the squires. Once the merchant families were established in their new class, they did their best to forget their origins.

*Anti-manufacturing snobbery*

The tradition of snobbism was transmitted intact to the new wealthy families of industrialists who rose on the tide of Britain's manufacturing supremacy of the nineteenth century ... Their ambition to adopt the habits and manners of their betters provided a splendid opportunity for alert educationists. Hence the proliferation of public boarding schools after the time of Thomas Arnold. The schools proved to be an effective instrument for bestowing gentility on the sons of the rough and warty industrial pioneers, and their vitality down to the present time can be attributed to the persistence of the same type of social ambition ...

*Strengths and faults of public schools* vis-à-vis *industry*

The public schools would not, of course, have flourished if they had not also served loftier purposes. They had great merits as the nursery of political leaders and administrators for several generations, and their products proved their mettle in the government of the British Empire ... In a word, the schools helped to form an elite, with the character and self-confidence appropriate to the needs of Britain as an imperial power ... The chief weakness of the schools ... was their failure to provide leaders equipped to manage Britain's economy in general, and her industry in particular, in an era when her former commercial supremacy was waning ...

*Failure of the universities to supply industrial leaders*

The inadequacy of school education in equipping the new generation of industrial leaders was not to be remedied by the universities. Despite the founding of the civic universities at the turn of the century, the higher education of the upper middle class was dominated by Oxford and Cambridge ... [which] had little interest in, or understanding of, industrial affairs ... The purpose of a university, it was held, was to make a 'whole man' and not to equip him to follow a specific calling, to prepare pupils for 'everything in general and nothing in particular' ...

*Vocational training in Continental countries*

On the Continent and in the USA, vocational training was held to be a proper function of a university. Nor was it considered inconsistent with the education of a cultivated citizen. A leader in business or administration was not thought to be inferior for having studied subjects relevant to the work he had to do ...

*The cult of the amateur*

... The English educational system was not open to criticism because it assigned a high place to the classics but simply because it left little room for anything else. Science and technology, in particular, were grossly neglected, a remarkable state of affairs when one considers the distinction of British scientists from the time of Bacon. This charge applies not only to the universities, but to English education as a whole ...

*Britain lagged behind in business education*

It was not only in the application of scientific knowledge to industry that Britain fell behind in the decades before 1914. The same was true of business education. The anti-intellectualist bias of British society, together with the prejudice against vocational education in the universities, was mainly responsible for Britain's long delay in introducing a system of training for the higher reaches of business comparable with that found among her commercial rivals ...

*The present day: Britain still lagging*

Now it may be objected that most of these criticisms relate to a period long past and that by the middle of the 1970s they applied only to a small and diminishing sector of industry. The dominion of the pre-war leaders was short and by the end of the 1950s new men had moved into positions of authority. Management had become more highly professionalised. The sources of recruitment had been augmented. Large firms had become accustomed to engage university graduates, not only those trained in science and technology, but also men with degrees in the arts and the social sciences for administrative work. In the 1960s Britain was at long last persuaded of the merits of a systematic academic training in business studies both at the graduate and postgraduate level.

*British industry still failing to attract graduates and professionals*
Even so, in comparison with other industrial countries, industry in Britain has not attracted a high proportion of the country's first-rate ability. The inclination of the best graduates is still to prefer an academic career, research, the civil service or the professions to jobs in industry ...

*Persisting cult of the amateur*
Despite the increasing professionalisation of management, the employment of highly trained scientists and technologists by many large businesses, and the substantial expenditure, public and private, on industrial and scientific research, the gap between Britain and her chief competitors in all but the last named activity has remained ...

G. C. Allen, *The British Disease: a Short Essay on the Nature and Causes of the Nation's Lagging Wealth* (Institute of Economic Affairs, Hobart Paper 67), London, 1979 (second edition), pp. 34–56.

## 5.6 Institutional constraints, 3: finance and industry

The view that manufacturing has been handicapped by the peculiarities of the British financial system, with the comparatively weak integration between finance and industry, has been a persistent theme in the discussion of British post-war economic performance.

Many of Britain's economic ills can be traced in whole or in part to the historic distortion in our credit system: the lowest rate of private sector investment in any OECD country, low output and productivity; a work force with low wages and morale – and aggravated inflation. The average life of all plant and machinery in Britain is thirty-five years – almost double that of France, Germany and the USA. This is not simply an hypothesis about what happens when credit is concentrated in certain ways. It is an observable reality ...

Our rivals have been selective for decades, channelling saving into investment rather than consumption. We have become less competitive and have gone on making ourselves more so by bouts of consumption-led reflation. Too much saving has gone to consumption, too little to investment, so that in every 'go' period in post-war Britain we have had consumption rising before the productive facilities are there to match it, greater imports as a consequence, inflationary bottlenecks and balance of payments deficits leading to the next 'stop', when, again, productive investment has been the first thing to be hit ...

If we are to create a benevolent instead of a malign dynamic we must by one means or another improve our investment ... Observation of the successful post-war economies, Japan and West Germany, produces these conclusions:

1. A much greater proportion of national product is reinvested. Britain's commercial and industrial companies' net investment is about 4 per cent of our GDP in the economic engine of plant and machinery. Japan normally invests 12 per cent net (France and West Germany run at about twice the UK rate). Our private sector net investment needs to be approximately doubled to match our partners in Europe, while for a Japanese rate of economic expansion our private sector investment needs to be more than trebled. Why have we fallen so far behind?

2. British industry has to try to raise most of its investment capital from its own profits. During the six years of 1974 to 1979 something like 70 per cent of the money for expansion came from within industry itself. In Japan, major finance comes from outside the company. The German entrepreneur is able to raise nearly three times as much money from the banks as the British.

3. Britain's banks lend comparatively little to industry. Japan's banks provide five times more money than Britain's for private sector investment. In Japan, bank loans to business amounted to something like 15 per cent of the national product between 1974 and 1978. In West Germany, the comparable figure is 8 per cent. In Britain, it is as low as 3 per cent.

4. Japan's industrialists have really long-term loans of fifteen to twenty years. In Germany, the formal term averages seven years and in Britain the formal term averages 2.5 years (it is more in practice as we shall discuss).

5. The league leaders in the world's productivity growth tables all have banking systems which make long-term loans to industry. The stock exchange and bond market, though they make a contribution, have never provided more than a small fraction of the external funds industry requires.

There is an index to describe and document this hidden dynamic behind Britain's decline. It is the debt-equity ratio, which displays the extent to which our industry is forced to rely on raising its own money. For every £100 a company borrows, the ratio says how much comes from outside the company (debt) and how much has been put up by the owners of the company (equity). Japan's debt-equity ratio is 85, Britain's is 22 ...

Our banking system has great integrity and the highest reputation but the principles on which it acts in Britain are not suited to business. The system works better in practice than the formal system since the average loan of 2.5 years is often allowed to roll over and the banks are usually prepared to lend more money to repay the original debt. But if the system works better than it might be thought to do, it works less well than it needs to do ...

The bank's sense of security is high in our system but it is bought at the expense of a sense of insecurity in the borrower which discourages risk-taking and expansion. A manufacturing entrepreneur in Britain contemplating expansion or innovation knows that when he goes to his bank he will usually be offered advances of two or three years or less and that they will not be allowed to exceed the 'gearing ratio' of one-third: he will not be advanced more than one-third of the asset value of his company. At the first tremor of difficulty in the economy he will be expected to give a good account of himself at his next bank interview ...

There is a further difficulty for the British entrepreneur. When his loan application is approved and his assets come to be valued, it will be in part on what they will fetch if he went bust rather than what they could earn as part of a going concern. Foreign bankers see the value of the company as a productive enterprise; British banks are apt to look at the carcass value. The small number of medium-term or long-term loans our banks advance are often only with property and other collateral, and that simply is not good enough for a venturesome society.

Harold Lever and George Edwards, 'Banking on Britain', *The Sunday Times*, 2 November 1980.

### 5.7 Anti-consensus, 1: the burden of the 'New Jerusalem'

This extract is taken from a published book, Correlli Barnett's *The Audit of War*, which received so much attention from politicians, press and public that it deserves to be considered as a 'document' in its own right. Barnett's analysis shares much in common with that of G. C. Allen (extract 5.5) but there is an added twist; Barnett argues that the British establishment came face-to-face with industrial shortcomings during the war and should have addressed these defects of British manufacturing. Instead, political leaders opted for stability and consensus in plans for a *welfare state*, or New Jerusalem, which ultimately proved too costly for the enfeebled industrial sector to bear.

The wartime coalition government therefore failed across the whole field of industrial and educational policy to evolve coherent medium- or long-term strategies capable of transforming Britain's obsolete industrial culture, and thereby working a British economic miracle. Instead all the boldness of vision, all the radical planning, all the lavishing of resources had gone towards working the *social* miracle of New Jerusalem.

Yet New Jerusalem was not the only wartime fantasy to beguile the British from a cold, clear vision of their true post-war priorities. Their political leaders and the governing Establishment, conditioned as they had been from their Edwardian childhoods to take it for granted that Britain stood in the first rank of nation states, simply could not accept that British power had vanished during the stupendous events of the second world war ... Instead they thought that Britain was suffering from mere short-term weaknesses in the wake of her wartime sacrifices; and they were resolved to restore and perpetuate Britain's traditional world role. The pursuit of this hallucination in the next quarter of a century was to cost Britain in defence expenditure up to double the proportion of GNP spent by European industrial competitors who limited themselves to contributing to the non-nuclear defence of the North Atlantic Treaty area. It was to impose a heavy dead weight on Britain's sluggish economy and on her fragile balance of payments, suck away from exports scarce manufacturing resources in advanced technology, and continue the wartime concentration of much of Britain's even scarcer R&D resources on defence projects.

And so it was that, by the time they took the bunting down from the streets after VE-Day[4] and turned from the war to the future, the British in their dreams and illusions and in their flinching from reality had already written the broad scenario for Britain's post-war descent into the place of fifth in the free world as an industrial power, with manufacturing output only two-fifths of West Germany's, and the place of fourteenth in the whole non-communist world in terms of annual GDP per head.

As that descent took its course the illusions and the dreams of 1945 would fade one by one – the imperial and Commonwealth role, the world power role, British industrial genius, and, at the last, New Jerusalem itself, a dream turned to a dank reality of a segregated, subliterate, unskilled, unhealthy and institutionalised proletariat hanging on the nipple of state maternalism.

Correlli Barnett, *The Audit of War: The Illusion and Reality of Britain as a Great Nation*, London, 1986, p. 304.

## 5.8 **Anti-consensus, 2: the view from the left**

Left-wing critics of the pattern of post-war development shared many of the insights of Barnett about the burden of the world role, the inability of the British establishment to modernise British industry, and the inability of an unmodernised industrial sector to support the 'welfare state'. The left also wanted state-led modernisation.

Since 1948 all British governments have followed virtual *laissez-faire* policies, refusing to plan the economy or to control trade. Under British conditions this has meant that balance of payments equilibrium can only be achieved by deflation at the cost of domestic unemployment and stagnation. This pattern of stop-go – short periods of growth followed by long periods of stagnation – has meant that there has been no sustained growth in demand and therefore no incentive for capitalism to invest. Low investment has meant that new techniques have been adopted slowly and productivity has lagged, so that British industry has become a depressed area of the EEC, requiring special help from more advanced countries ...

The determined state intervention in investment, production and trade necessary to break out of this vicious circle has been opposed by capitalists because it would pose a very grave political threat. Britain is a country with a powerful working class with long socialist traditions. The position of capital is never secure and the ruling class maintains its position partly by the ideological weapon of praising the private sector and denigrating the nationalised industries and the public sector as a whole. This weapon would be seriously blunted by a successful policy of state-directed modernisation, even if carried through by a Tory government. It would be clear to all that planning, unlike the market mechanism, was able to attain national economic objectives ... The dilemma of British capitalism is that, economically speaking, it requires determined state intervention, but quite correctly (from its own point of view) it fears the political consequences.

The Cambridge Political Economy Group, *Britain's Economic Crisis*, Spokesman Pamphlet 44, Nottingham 1974, pp. 7–8.

## 5.9 Anti-consensus, 3: too much union power

The author, Sir Keith Joseph, was a key Minister in both the Heath and Thatcher Conservative governments. His place in history is, however, likely to be as one of the leading figures in bringing monetarist and neoclassical economic ideas back into British politics.

The walls of our economic prison are closing in upon us, because all our social and economic problems reinforce each other. We don't have unlimited time, because each year the problem gets harder, the prison cell smaller ...

There are many big and difficult things we have to do if we are to escape from the trap. We have to hold and then reduce government's share of national spending and abate inflation. Just as important, we have to remove the fears that inflation will soar again. We have to work out a systematic approach to pay determination in the non-market public sector ... We have to reduce the present power of the trade unions to damage the economy and at the same time reduce the pressures which encourage them to do so.

Each of these objectives, and there are many others, is an immense task. Each is an exercise in analysis, innovation, persuasion and co-operation. And when they are all achieved, they give us no more than a stable platform on which to build, in place of today's slow disintegration. They give us a few stepping stones on the way to national recovery.

The first of these stepping stones must be the replacement of the militants' charter by a moderates' charter ... We say that union power should be reduced, not because we are 'anti-union', nor because we think it is the sole cause of our problems, but because the present imbalance of power bars our way to national recovery.

Sir Keith Joseph, *Solving the Union Problem is the Key to Britain's Recovery* (Centre for Policy Studies pamphlet), London, 1979.

## 5.10 Anti-consensus, 4: lack of competitive pressure

In this extract Nick Crafts argues that the period of consensus policies induced cosy collusion between economic agents which produced a rate of output and productivity growth well below what should have been possible.

The consequences for bargained productivity outcomes,[5] of soft budget constraints[6] and lack of competition were most vividly seen in the British nationalised industries which accounted for about 20 per cent of all investment. [There have been] major problems resulting from lax government control in which politicians' incentives were to condone and conceal over-manning and over-investment. Reports by the Monopolies and Mergers Commission in the early 1980s were severely critical of long records of misuse of manpower and capital in both coal ... and electricity ... The table confirms the poor productivity performance of the 1970s and shows the improvements of the 1980s. Then, in the still nationalised coal and steel sectors, government reformed productivity by putting itself in the new position of accepting plant closures, setting credible financial targets and acting to enhance its bargaining power *vis-à-vis* both management and unions.

Successive governments sought co-operation with the TUC and placed a high priority on saving jobs, especially in the regions. Perhaps it is not therefore surprising to find [one] assessment of the industrial policies of the 1960s and 1970s as 'directed at helping old industries to survive rather than encouraging new products and new technology' ... The early post-war years were a period in which import penetration was low and many industries were collusive ... Moreover, although hostile take-overs emerged as a threat to sleepy management, the evidence strongly suggests that the merger and take-over boom of the 1960s did little in practice to raise productivity growth or discriminate effectively against the incompetent manager ...

**Productivity outcomes in the UK nationalised/privatised sector**

| | *Labour productivity growth (% p.a.)* | | *Mid–1970s relative labour productivity level* | |
|---|---|---|---|---|
| | *1968–78* | *1978–88* | *WG/UK* | *USA/UK* |
| Coal | –0.7 | 6.2 | 2.64 | 7.60 |
| Railways | 0.8 | 0.8 | 1.08 | 3.95 |
| Steel | –0.2 | 9.4 | 1.52 | 2.57 |
| Electricity | 5.3 | 3.2 | 2.25 | 3.47 |
| Postal | –1.3 | 2.2 | 1.07 | 2.28 |
| Gas | 8.5 | 5.2 | 2.23 | 2.79 |
| Telecom | 8.2 | 5.6 | 1.07 | 2.69 |
| Airways | 6.4 | 4.2 | 1.59 | 1.52 |
| National Freight | 2.7 | 3.7 | 1.27 | 1.80 |

In sum, the evidence is that a good deal of the relatively slow growth of the UK during the 'Golden Age'[7] was due to an environment which permitted or even encouraged the survival of the inefficient and created a situation where the bargaining power of those seeking to block productivity-enhancing change was often considerable. Britain's less rapid catching up of the USA reflects institutional differences. New growth economics[8] offers insights into but by no means a full account of the growth gap between the UK and Germany while its apparent policy prescription of subsidy to investment is seen to have been unhelpful.

*A renaissance in the 1980s?*
If the preceding account is correct, it implies that a policy configuration which changed bargaining power through raising unemployment, increasing competition and making firms' budget constraints tighter and harder would potentially have a substantial impact on productivity growth, at least during a transitional period until a new equilibrium was established. The change in policy regime and external shocks of the early 1980s provided a new economic environment along these lines.

N. F. R. Crafts, *Can De-industrialisation seriously Damage your Wealth? A Review of why Growth Rates differ and how to improve Economic Performance* (Institute of Economic Affairs, Hobart Paper 120), London, 1993, pp. 47–9.

## 5.11 The last word on growth – from an economist

Paul Ormerod, one of the country's leading economic forecasters, looks back on thirty years of progress in economics. He suggests that economists have *no* convincing answers to the following four questions. Why has unemployment risen so strongly in the past twenty years? Why has the unemployment experience of Western countries been so diverse? What determines growth in the long term? What will be the output of the British economy twelve months hence?

Over the past thirty years or so, economic theory is littered with new concepts that have given very little insight into how economies actually work. This theoretical work was done in a vacuum, tightly insulated from empirical evidence ... [For example,] from the late 1950s to the early 1970s, the theory of economic growth was very fashionable in economics. Many of the most powerful intellects in the profession devoted themselves to work in this area. Yet it is not being unduly harsh to say that the whole corpus of this work has left virtually nothing of value to a policy-maker who wishes to understand how growth in his or her economy can be stimulated in the long term ...

The ability to predict events is a fundamental test of the validity of any scientific approach to the world. Yet, far from progressing as theoretical economics expands, the forecasting record of models, never brilliant, has deteriorated since the mid–1980s. In virtually every Western country, serious errors have been made in forecasts. The example of the UK in the past few years is clear.

Most economists scorn applied work and are content to build elaborate theoretical models whose empirical foundations may be non-existent. Those who do try to forecast have found it very difficult to generate accurate predictions at the macroeconomic level.

The basic approach of economics should be to seek to explain observed phenomena. Theory should in general follow observation, rather than the highly abstract approach that prevails at present. Economists need to be far more eclectic in their use of techniques from other disciplines. In particular, they should recognise that human society corresponds much more to a self-organising system, in which behaviour adapts over time, and which from time to time suffers external shocks, than to the nineteenth-century mechanical view of the world that pervades the discipline at present.

Paul Ormerod, 'Waiting for Newton', *New Statesman and Society*, 28 August 1992, p. 13.

# Notes

## Introduction

1 N. F. R. Crafts, for example, argues that the period of relative decline spans the full century before 1979: *Can De-industrialisation seriously Damage your Wealth? A Review of why Growth Rates differ and how to improve Economic Performance*, London, 1993, pp. 18–20. Sidney Pollard, on the other hand, singles out the period since 1950 as the problem years: *The Wasting of the British Economy*, London, second edition 1982, pp. 1–14. A third position is taken by Barry Supple, who argues that Britain has declined relatively but has continued to grow at a rate which is consistent with its resources, aptitudes, institutions and attitudes: 'British economic decline since 1945' in R. Floud and D. N. McCloskey, eds., *The Economic History of Britain since 1700: 3, 1939–92*, Cambridge, second edition 1994.

2 Angus Maddison, *Phases of Capitalist Development*, Oxford, 1982; *idem*, *Dynamic Forces in Capitalist Development: A Long-run Comparative View*, Oxford, 1991.

3 R. C. O. Matthews, C. H. Feinstein and J. C. Odling-Smee, *British Economic Growth, 1856–1973*, Oxford, 1982.

4 Mancur Olson, *The Rise and Decline of Nations: Economic Growth, Stagnation and Social Rigidities*, New Haven, Conn., 1982.

5 The other main imported institutional approach is found in B. Elbaum and W. Lazonick, eds., *The Decline of the British Economy*, Oxford, 1986. The critique from domestic economic and social historians may be gathered in M. W. Kirby, 'Institutional rigidities and economic decline: reflections on the British experience', *Economic History Review*, XLV, 1992, pp. 637–60.

6 The leading contributions to the convergence thesis are: M. Abramovitz, 'Catching up, forging ahead and falling behind', *Journal of Economic History*, XLVI, 1986, pp. 385–406, and W. J. Baumol, 'Productivity growth, convergence and welfare: what the long-run data show', *American Economic Review*, LXXVI, 1986, pp. 1072–85.

7 R. Bacon and W. Eltis, *Britain's Economic Problem: Too Few Producers*, London, 1976.
8 See, in particular, two articles by David Metcalf: 'Water notes dry up: the impact of the Donovan reforms and Thatcherism at work on labour productivity in British manufacturing industry', *British Journal of Industrial Relations*, XXVII, 1989, pp. 1–31; 'Union presence and labour productivity in British manufacturing industry: a reply to Nolan and Marginson', *British Journal of Industrial Relations*, XXVIII, 1990, pp. 249–66.
9 M. M. Postan, *An Economic History of Western Europe, 1945–1964*, London, 1967.
10 The hypothesis was first developed by J. C. R. Dow in *The Management of the British Economy, 1945–60*, Cambridge, 1964.
11 This approach is most closely associated with the economist A. P. Thirlwall and is most clearly set out in 'The balance of payments constraint as an explanation of international growth rate differences', *Banco del Lavoro Quarterly Review*, CXXVIII, 1979, pp. 44–53.
12 Sidney Pollard, *The Development of the British Economy, 1914–1960*, London, 1962.
13 C. F. Pratten, *Labour Productivity Differentials within International Companies*, Cambridge, 1976; S. J. Prais, *Productivity and Industrial Structure: A Statistical Study of Manufacturing Industry in Britain, Germany and the United States*, Cambridge, 1981; S. Davies and R. E. Caves, *Britain's Productivity Gap*, Cambridge, 1987.
14 See note 4 above.
15 See note 5 above.
16 The literature is surveyed in C. F. Pratten and A. G. Atkinson, 'The use of manpower in British manufacturing industry', *Department of Employment Gazette*, LXXXIV, 1976, pp. 571–6.
17 French growth was assisted throughout the long boom by the determination of the government to devalue to give French exporters a competitive edge in external markets. As French industrialists came to rely on government action along these lines, the budgets of French firms were correspondingly soft. Nevertheless, Tables 1 and 4 show by how much the French economy outperformed the British during the long boom. The soft budgets of German firms arose less from government action than from the complementary nature of Germany's producer and basic industries with the consumer goods industries of her European neighbours. Competition from other producers was weak.
18 In part because the resources released by manufacturing have flowed into low productivity services, where the pace of productivity growth has slowed because of the lavish supply of labour available to employers.

## *Notes*

### Chapter 1

1 Britain suffered a substantial fall in the value of its overseas investments during the second world war. See extract 2.1 for details.
2 1950–55 and 1955–60.
3 The elasticity of demand for imports is the amount by which imports will rise following a given rise in British incomes. The concept is discussed above in the introduction, pp. 30–1.
4 The terms of trade are the ratio of an index of export prices to an index of import prices. The terms of trade improve either if export prices rise more quickly than import prices or if export prices fall more slowly than import prices. A favourable shift in the terms of trade enabled Britain to purchase more imports with a given quantity of exports, thus increasing welfare.
5 The National Economic Development Council which established a target rate of growth of 4 per cent per annum.
6 The stop-go cycle is discussed in the Introduction; see above, p. 30.
7 In their book *Britain's Economic Problem: Too Few Producers*, London, 1976 (which is now widely regarded as having been mistaken).
8 Not an easy concept to define unambiguously. Extract 2.10 raises the problems, but then rather overlooks them.
9 In short, Britain would export capital to purchase assets in other countries which would supply a stream of interest and dividend income to replace that lost from the export earnings of British manufacturing. Her analysis was remarkably accurate.
10 Which, of course, do not correspond to trade cycle peaks and therefore do include distortion by cyclical factors.
11 It all depends how one defines 'a declining manufacturing base'. If absolute output of manufacturing is the focus, the base did not decline. If the output of manufacturing relative to other sectors of the economy is the focus, the manufacturing base did decline.
12 Asset price inflation is simply the rise in price of financial and physical assets, which was particularly rapid in the later 1980s. Excessive private sector debt levels represented the indebtedness incurred by consumers in the purchase of housing and other goods and by the business sector to finance new investment, company acquisitions or other motives.
13 The G–5 are the five economically most powerful countries (or more exactly the four most powerful plus Britain). They have now become the G–7.
14 The savings ratio is the proportion of income which is saved, usually expressed for personal savings as the proportion of disposable income (i.e. household income after tax and national insurance contributions

have been deducted). In the post-war period the savings ratio has risen steadily from approximately 2 per cent in the late 1940s to 13 per cent in 1980, whereupon it fell, as the extract indicates.

15 As a result of bigger interest payments at the higher interest rates.

16 Indebtedness had increased and savings had fallen, as noted above in the extract, but unemployment also rose, hitting household income very hard for those who lost their employment.

17 Gearing is the ratio of a firm's borrowing to the value of its assets. See extract 5.6 for an example of the use of the term.

18 Those goods and services which can be sold overseas.

## Chapter 2

1 Output per man-shift – the coal industry's traditional measure of labour productivity.

2 Nationalisation of the industry had been on and off the political agenda since the first world war but had become particularly contentious since 1942.

3 The right to exploit underground minerals belonged to the owners of the land at the surface and this, as the extract makes clear, will not necessarily result in economically rational development of underground mineral resources.

4 The throughways from the shaft to the face.

5 Resulting from the devastation of war. Starvation was a very real threat, especially for the displaced persons of Europe. Even in Britain, food rationing was worse in many respects after the war than during it.

6 A variety of schemes were adopted. Displaced persons were encouraged to come and work in British industry, and European volunteer workers were recruited for specific industries (agriculture, textiles, coal mining).

7 In the USA very few unions used work study engineers. This was one of the many myths which the AACP helped to create.

8 The missing paragraphs all deal with detailed technical improvements.

9 The action plans were drawn up in tripartite discussions to enable each industry to expand its output in conformity with the requirements of faster overall growth in the National Plan.

10 The cost of model development began to rise in the 1970s as a result of controls over vehicle exhaust emissions and the need to develop more fuel-efficient engines after the huge rises in oil prices in 1973–74.

11 The British Leyland Motor Corporation, formed by the merger in 1968 of British Motor Holdings (dominated by Austin and Morris) with the Leyland Motor Corporation (which had been based in heavy goods

vehicle production – Leyland, AEC, Albion – but had diversified into motor car manufacture – Rover, Standard, Triumph).

12 A report commissioned by the Secretary of State for Industry (Tony Benn) in December 1974, when it became clear that BLMC would collapse without government support.

13 The Society of Motor Manufacturers and Traders.

14 Pat Lowry, b. 1920. Director of Personnel and Industrial Relations of BLMC, 1975–77; subsequently chair of ACAS, 1981–87. Knighted in 1985.

15 Moss Evans, b. 1925. National Organiser, Transport and General Workers' Union,1973–78; General Secretary, 1978–85. Member, TUC General Council, 1977–85.

16 Resulting from the sale to foreigners of services supplied by British firms.

17 In the event, 1973 proved to be the rule, not the exception, and 1974 was a 'rogue' year. Britons have a high propensity to take foreign holidays, and net receipts on the tourism account have been much less dynamic than appeared likely in the early 1970s.

18 Research and development.

19 Newly industrialised country.

20 Organisation of Petroleum Exporting Countries.

21 Currency held by institutions and individuals outside the country of issue. Eurodollars were the first such currency and arose when US banks chose to move some of their operations to Europe to escape the constraints imposed by the Federal Reserve System. Eurocurrency markets have grown rapidly since the mid–1960s.

22 Judgements on the performance of foreign-owned 'transplants' has not always been so favourable. There has been criticism in the recent past that some of these foreign-owned plant are merely assembling kits of parts which have been made elsewhere. In the 1970s there were very robust criticisms of the failure of foreign-owned multinationals to invest in their UK operations and of their ability to evade control by national governments.

23 After the article had appeared Rover was sold into German (BMW) ownership and Rolls-Royce concluded a major sourcing and development agreement with another German motor manufacturer, Mercedes-Benz.

24 Service sector productivity growth is probably underestimated because statisticians need to split the revenue of service sector companies into changes in output and changes in prices to begin to measure productivity. However, it is extremely difficult to make proper allowance for increases in quality within this calculation, and many economists believe that service sector output, and hence service sector productivity, is underestimated.

## Chapter 3

1 Lend-lease was the scheme under which the US government provided its allies with defence material of any kind (armaments, ships, food) anywhere in the world, without cash payment, for 'purposes essential to the defence of the United States'. The UK also made resources available to the US government, under what was known as reverse lend-lease, but the flow was overwhelmingly from the USA to the UK.

2 The counterpart of lend-lease and reverse lend-lease in Anglo-Canadian relations.

3 See the entry in the glossary at the end of this volume.

4 The day of victory in the war against Japan.

5 One of a series of pledges which culminated in the formation of NATO on 4 April 1949.

6 The International Trade Organisation, which was expected to fulfil the role of overseeing world trade, much as the International Monetary Fund was to oversee in world payments. The ITO was, however, not ratified, and instead a less ambitious General Agreement on Tariffs and Trade has monitored and managed world trade (see extract 3.4).

7 Allowing sterling to be freely convertible into other currencies, especially the dollar. The premature adoption of convertibility was one of the factors in the foreign exchange crisis of 1947.

8 The European Recovery Programme, more commonly known as Marshall Aid.

9 The Organisation for European Economic Co-operation, established on 16 April 1948 to co-ordinate the European response to the offer of Marshall Aid. It has subsequently become the OECD, the Organisation for Economic Co-operation and Development.

10 A customs union is an agreement between two or more countries which allows free internal trade between members of the union and imposes a common external tariff on all members. The most famous customs union is the European Union. It should be contrasted with a free-trade area, which also allows free trade between members but allows each member to retain its own distinctive tariff structure.

11 Paul-Henri Spaak, 1899–1972. Belgian Prime Minister and Foreign Minister, 1948–51. Foreign Minister, 1954–57, 1961–56.

12 A scheme established by the seventeen members of the OEEC in 1950 to liberalise payments between members and supply credits to any member in balance of payments deficit.

13 A political veto on devaluation (known as the 'great unmentionable' in government circles) had operated from the time when the government came to office until devaluation actually took place.

14 The 1949 devaluation, in which Harold Wilson had played a prominent role, had been aimed primarily at altering quite drastically

the sterling-dollar relationship, with a cut of approximately 30 per cent in sterling's relative value. However, most of the non-dollar world followed Britain, and the overall effect of Britain's devaluation, after all other currency changes had been made and weighted by the distribution of Britain's trade, was no more than 9 per cent. In effect, the rest of the world devalued against the US dollar.

15 The Chancellor of the Exchequer's budget speech on 21 March 1972 had announced that Britain would not allow the regime of pegged exchange rates to thwart domestic expansion as it had under the stop-go pattern.

16 Public Sector Borrowing Requirement, the amount by which public expenditure exceeds government revenue.

17 President Johnson almost certainly behaved as Denis Healey has described, but it was under Johnson's successor, Richard Nixon, that the era of Bretton Woods finally ended.

18 Under ERM arrangements, member currencies have a central rate but are allowed to fluctuate within a margin either side of the central rate. Sterling's value could fluctuate by 6 per cent either side of its central rate. So the floor rate was substantially below the central rate.

## Chapter 4

1 This was rather disingenuous. The cost of living index was known to be in urgent need of revision because it was so unrepresentative of working-class purchasing patterns. The official index understated the true rate of price rises by a considerable margin.

2 Under the 'concentration of production' scheme, the production of a number of industries which had been reduced by government order during the early phases of war was concentrated into a limited number of firms, so as to maximise the release of labour and storage space for more productive use in the war economy. The policy came into operation in March 1941.

3 During the 1950s trade unionists were highly concerned about the impact of new continuous production methods on worker fatigue.

4 R. A. Butler, 1902–82. Conservative MP for Saffron Walden, 1929–65. Chancellor of the Exchequer, 1951–55; Lord Privy Seal, 1955–59; Home Secretary, 1957–62; Deputy Prime Minister, 1962–63. Life peerage 1965: Lord Butler of Saffron Walden.

5 Sir Graham Hayman, 1897–1983. Director of various industrial companies, 1927–65. Chair of the Distillers Company Ltd, 1958–63, and of British Plaster Board (Holdings) Ltd, 1956–65. President of the Federation of British Industries, 1955–57.

6 Charles Geddes, 1897–1983. General Secretary of the Union of Post Office Workers, 1944–57. Member of the TUC General Council,

1946–57. President of the TUC, 1954–55. Life peerage 1958: Lord Geddes of Epsom.

7 Wilfred Heywood, 1900–77. General Secretary of the National Union of Dyers, Bleachers and Textile Workers, and member of the TUC General Council, 1948–57.

8 Sir Vincent Tewson, 1898–1977. Assistant General Secretary, TUC, 1931–46. General Secretary, 1946–60.

9 There was a 'bulge' in the birth rate immediately after the war and by the early 1960s these 'baby boomers' were beginning to emerge on to the labour market.

10 Regional policy was an essential part of growth strategies in the 1960s, with the aim of re-locating firms to where supplies of labour were more plentiful and so allowing expansion to take place with less likelihood of inflation. However, the programme misunderstood the stimuli to inflation and ignored the extra costs of firms in sub-optimal locations.

11 Part-time is defined officially as less than thirty hours per week with the result that differences between full- and part-time work have narrowed as the length of the normal working week has fallen.

12 Unemployed for more than one year.

13 This process is known as 'hysteresis'.

## Chapter 5

1 The consolidated railway timetable, published every year until nationalization made it unnecessary.

2 Colleges of Advanced Technology, which subsequently became technological universities.

3 The reorganisers of the British civil service in the mid-nineteenth century.

4 The day on which victory was secured over Germany.

5 The negotiations over wages and effort.

6 When expansion of the macro-economy (allegedly) allows firms to make mistakes over prices, methods of production, quality of final product and still escape bankruptcy because of the pressure of general demand. See the reservations expressed in the Introduction, pp. 35–6.

7 The long boom in the world economy from 1951 to 1973.

8 Models of growth in which faster rates of accumulation of physical capital equipment or human capital can lead to persistently higher rates of growth of output without being offset by diminishing returns.

# Glossary of economic terms

**capacity utilisation** The extent to which available supplies of labour and capital are fully employed in producing economic output. The extent of capacity utilisation is usually measured by the proportion of the total labour force in employment.

**demand side** In macroeconomics, the main categories of demand are consumers' expenditure on goods and services, investment in capital goods and stocks, and the foreign balance (exports of goods and services less expenditure on imports of goods and services).

**growth accounting** The method of seeking to understand the proximate causes of growth of output by measuring the contribution to output change of the different factors of production (land, labour and capital) and of the efficiency with which those factors are used in the production process (total factor productivity). The method is highly controversial because of empirical problems (the proportions of the different factor inputs do not remain constant over time and their individual contribution to output change is difficult to disentangle), conceptual difficulties (in order for the sources of growth to be attributed accurately between factor inputs and total factor productivity, the method has to make very strong assumptions about the nature of the economic system which are very far from being satisfied by modern economies) and interpretative analysis (the method can show only the proximate sources of growth and cannot demonstrate why factor inputs or total factor productivity have changed over time).

**macroeconomic** Relating to the whole economic system and, when used in Keynesian economics, to the theory of income determination, which is the way which the components of aggregate demand (see 'demand side' above) affect national income.

**microeconomic** The study of economics at the level of the individual consumer, groups of consumers or firms.

**national product** The net value of all economic goods and services produced in the country in a given period, usually one year. Economic goods are those which are produced for gain, though economic statisticians apply broad conventions to decide precisely what is an economic good. Only the net value of final goods is included, so the value of intermediate goods (raw materials, component parts, etc.) is assumed to be used up in the production of final goods and services and is not counted.

**petro-currency** A currency the value of which is heavily influenced by the changing price of oil in world markets.

**purchasing power parities** Experience has shown that the use of official exchange rates to convert the value of the national product of one country into the currency of another gives misleading results. The official exchange rate is influenced by the prices of goods which are traded, but many goods and services do not enter into international trade. The purchasing power parity method seeks to overcome these limitations by seeking from direct observation to measure the comparative value of currencies, including both traded and non-traded goods and services.

**real living standards** National income per head of the population, after adjustment for changes in price levels.

**stagflation** The simultaneous existence of rising unemployment and rising inflation. The Keynesian theory which dominated British economics in the post-war years held that either inflation or unemployment would be rising, as there was a direct trade-off between the two (more of one necessarily meant less of the other).

**sterling area countries** A group of countries which tied the value of their domestic currency to sterling and used sterling to settle international balances of payments. The group was loosely formed in the aftermath of Britain's abandonment of the gold standard in 1931, but became much more formalised with the introduction of exchange controls during the second world war. The size of the sterling area gradually diminished after sterling's devaluation in 1967 and especially after the floating of the pound in 1972.

**supply side** Those factors which affect the behaviour of individual workers and firms. Supply side economics as practised in the UK and USA has both a negative and a positive side. The negative side denies a role to Keynesian-style macroeconomic management, which it believes will change the inflation rate but will leave real variables essentially unchanged. More positively, supply side economists believe that they can improve the performance of the national economy by measures to increase the exposure of firms and workers to market forces, increasing the flexibility of workers and firms and increasing incentives to higher effort.

**trade cycle** Regular fluctuations in the level of national income. Each trade cycle will have a peak and a trough.

**underlying growth rate** The rate of change of the productive potential of the economy; in other words, long-term changes in national income which exclude the effects of the trade cycle.

# Guide to further reading

Students of recent economic history are poorly served by volumes of primary sources. The main collection, Pope and Hoyle's *British Economic Performance, 1880–1980*, London, 1985, has an excellent range of material on the evolution of British industry and also contains a short statistical appendix. It does, however, cover the whole century after 1880 and therefore the amount of space devoted to post-war performance is inevitably rather limited. Relevant material will also be found in two volumes edited by Coates and Hilliard, *The Economic Decline of Modern Britain: The Debate between Left and Right*, Brighton, 1986, and *The Economic Revival of Modern Britain: The Debate between Left and Right*, Aldershot, 1987. As the titles indicate, the coverage is mainly of the politics of economic policy, especially in the period since 1970, but there is much of interest in both volumes. Those brave souls who intend to search out their own primary source material should equip themselves with C. L. Mowat, *Great Britain since 1914*, London 1970, which is a rather dated but nonetheless useful guide to primary sources for twentieth-century historians. It was designed to be used mainly by students of political history, but economic historians will also find instructive and perceptive guidance.

As far as secondary sources are concerned, there has been an explosion in recent years of studies of the British economy since 1945, but the level of economic sophistication required to understand much of this output is well beyond that which can be reasonably expected of A-level and first-year undergraduate students in economic and social history. As a result, there is no useful introductory text which concentrates exclusively on the whole period since the war. The best starting place is B. W. E. Alford, *British Economic Performance, 1945–1975*, London, 1988. For those wishing to place the post-war period into a rather longer perspective, Michael Dintenfass, *The Decline of Industrial Britain, 1870–1980*, London, 1992, is a beautifully written, compact study which focuses on the contribution of institutional and cultural factors in Britain's relative decline. The best quarry for those with more narrowly economic interests remains Sidney

Pollard's *The Development of the British Economy, 1914–1990*, London, 1993. Those with the appetite and the confidence to tackle the literature which has been more ostentatiously influenced by changing currents within economic theory should select chapters from the volume edited by Nick Crafts and Nick Woodward, *The British Economy since 1945*, Oxford, 1991; the chapters on growth (by Crafts), inflation (by Woodward), and the balance of payments (by Foreman-Peck) are reasonably accessible. In a similar vein, Prest and Coppock's *The UK Economy: A Manual of Applied Economics*, London, 1992 (the thirteenth edition, now edited by M. J. Artis) contains much that will be of great benefit to non-economists. D. Morris, ed., *The Economic System in the UK*, Oxford, 1985, was conceived as a course in applied economics for non-specialists and contains a chapter on economic growth by Christopher Allsopp which is highly recommended. Finally, the second edition of Roderick Floud and D. N. McCloskey, eds., *The Economic History of Britain since 1700*, Cambridge, 1994, now has a separate volume (Volume III) devoted to the period since 1939. To supplement these (largely) macroeconomic treatments, A-level and first-year undergraduate students can extract a lot of very useful information and analysis from three essentially microeconomic approaches: Karel Williams, John Williams and Dennis Thomas, *Why are the British bad at Manufacturing?* London, 1983, Roy Church, *The Rise and Decline of the British Motor Industry*, London, 1994, and Howard Gospel, *Markets, Firms and the Management of Labour in Modern Britain*, Cambridge, 1992. Finally, two efforts to explain the British disease in terms of cultural influences have provoked enormous interest. Both Martin Wiener, *English Culture and the Decline of the Industrial Spirit*, Cambridge, 1981, and Correlli Barnett, *The Audit of War: The Illusion and Reality of Britain as a Great Nation*, London, 1986, struck a chord with educated British opinion though economic historians have tended to be underwhelmed by both arguments, as may be gathered from the final chapter of Michael Dintenfass's book cited above and from W. D. Rubinstein, *Capitalism, Culture and Decline in Britain, 1750–1990*, London, 1993. Thus the range of possible explanations of the British disease is enormous. There is simply no consensus about which is most convincing.

# Index